Gooseberry Patch

Slow Cookers, Casseroles & Skillets

D1314580

Gooseberry Patch
600 London Road
P.O. Box 190
Delaware, OH 43015

www.gooseberrypatch.com

1·800·854·6673

Copyright 2010, Gooseberry Patch 978-1-936283-00-2
Third Printing, July, 2010

Do you have a tried & true recipe...
tip, craft or memory that you'd like to see featured in a **Gooseberry
Patch** cookbook? Visit our website at **www.gooseberrypatch.com**,
register and follow the easy steps to submit your favorite family recipe.
Or send them to us at:

Gooseberry Patch
Attn: Cookbook Dept.
P.O. Box 190
Delaware, OH 43015

Don't forget to include the number of servings your recipe makes,
plus your name, address, phone number and email address.
If we select your recipe, your name will appear right along
with it...and you'll receive a **FREE** copy of the cookbook!

Contents

Dedication

To everyone who enjoys the simple pleasure of a flavorful home-cooked meal.

Appreciation

To all of you who shared your tastiest, most family-friendly recipes with us.

Savory Slow Cookers

Snowstorm Beef Stew

Helen Burns
Raleigh, NC

This recipe's ingredient list may seem a little unusual! I came up with it during a winter storm, using what we had in the pantry and freezer. We've enjoyed this stew ever since.

2 lbs. stew beef, cubed
18-1/2 oz. can French onion
  soup
16-oz. container sour cream
  onion dip

2 13-1/4 oz. cans mixed
  vegetables, drained
7-oz. pkg. elbow macaroni,
  uncooked and divided

Place beef in a slow cooker; pour soup over top. Cover and cook on high setting for 3 hours. Stir in dip; cover and cook for an additional 2 hours, stirring occasionally. Add vegetables and one cup uncooked macaroni, reserving the rest of macaroni for another recipe. Cover and cook on high setting for one additional hour, or until macaroni is tender. Makes 4 to 6 servings.

Let everyone know what's for dinner tonight! Paint "Mom's Menu" on an old-fashioned slate chalkboard and set it next to the slow cooker.

Pennsylvania Stuffed Peppers

Lora Burek
Irwin, PA

The perfect comfort food...they taste even better the next day! Mashed potatoes are heavenly topped with some of the sauce from the peppers.

1-1/2 lbs. ground beef
1 egg, beaten
1 c. orzo pasta or instant rice,
   uncooked
garlic salt and pepper to taste

6 green, yellow or red peppers,
   tops removed
2 10-3/4 oz. cans tomato soup
2-1/2 c. water

Mix beef, egg, uncooked orzo or rice and seasonings in a bowl. Stuff peppers lightly with mixture. If any extra beef mixture remains, form into small meatballs. In a slow cooker, blend together soup and water. Arrange stuffed peppers in slow cooker; replace tops on peppers for a nice touch. Place meatballs around peppers. Lightly spoon some of soup mixture onto tops of peppers. Cover and cook on low setting for 8 to 10 hours. Serves 6.

Keep most-used recipes at your fingertips! Tack them to self-stick cork tiles placed inside a kitchen cabinet door.

Country-Style Scalloped Potatoes
Eleanor Paternoster
Bridgeport, CT

Old-fashioned flavor...fix & forget convenience!

6 russet potatoes, thinly sliced
1-1/2 lbs. ham steak, cubed
10-3/4 oz. can cream of
   mushroom soup

1-1/4 c. water
1 c. shredded Cheddar cheese
grill seasoning to taste

Layer potatoes and ham in a slow cooker that has been sprayed with non-stick vegetable spray. Combine remaining ingredients; pour over potatoes and ham. Cover and cook on high setting for 3-1/2 hours, until potatoes are fork-tender. Turn slow cooker to low setting; continue cooking for about one hour. Makes 4 to 6 servings.

Post a dinner wishlist on the fridge and invite everyone to jot down their favorite dishes. Family members who are involved in meal planning are much more likely to look forward to family dinnertimes together.

Cheesy Parmesan Polenta

Marian Buckley
Fontana, CA

This creamy dish makes a great alternative to pasta or potatoes. I like to serve it topped with my favorite homemade mushroom spaghetti sauce...yum! You'll find polenta next to regular cornmeal at the grocery store.

9 c. chicken broth
1/4 c. butter, sliced
1 bay leaf

3 c. instant polenta, uncooked
3 c. grated Parmesan cheese

In a saucepan over medium heat, bring broth, butter and bay leaf to a boil. Gradually whisk in polenta; add cheese and continue whisking until well blended. Transfer to a slow cooker. Cover and cook on low setting for 25 to 30 minutes. Discard bay leaf before serving. Serves 6.

Make mealtime extra special with cloth napkins.
Glue wooden alphabet letter initials to plain napkin rings...
pretty place settings too!

Vegetable Beef Soup

Colleen Pancari
Vineland, NJ

Every country kitchen should have an easy, delicious recipe
for vegetable beef soup...this is mine!

1 lb. stew beef, cubed
3 14-1/2 oz. cans beef broth
2 16-oz. pkgs. frozen mixed
   vegetables

14-1/2 oz. can whole tomatoes
16-oz. pkg. wide egg noodles,
   uncooked and divided

Combine all ingredients except noodles in a slow cooker. Cover and cook on low setting for 4 hours. Increase to high setting; cover and cook for 5 additional hours. About 20 minutes before serving, stir in half the noodles, or desired amount, reserving the rest for another recipe. Cover and cook an additional 15 to 20 minutes, until noodles are tender. Serves 4 to 6.

Convert your favorite stovetop soup recipe to fix & forget in a slow cooker. Most soups that simmer for one to 2 hours will be done in 8 to 10 hours on low or 4 to 5 hours on high. Wait until the last 30 minutes to add dairy ingredients like sour cream and tender veggies like peas.

Hearty Lasagna Soup

Marcia Bills
Orleans, NE

My daughters request this soup whenever they are coming home from college for weekends or holidays...in fact, our family calls it Coming Home Soup! It's so warm and delicious...we all love it.

1 lb. ground beef, browned and drained
6.4-oz. pkg. ground beef lasagna dinner, divided

6 c. water
1 c. corn
15-oz. can Italian-style stewed tomatoes

Place beef in a slow cooker. Add lasagna sauce mix, water, corn and undrained tomatoes; stir well. Cover and cook on low setting for 4 to 6 hours. Mix in lasagna noodles and cook an additional 20 minutes, until noodles are tender. Makes 6 servings.

Bake some savory garlic twists for dinner. Separate refrigerated bread stick dough and lay flat on an ungreased baking sheet. Brush with olive oil; sprinkle with garlic salt and dried parsley. Give each bread stick a twist or two and bake as directed on the package.

Creamy Mushroom Chicken

Kathy Tormaschy
Richardton, ND

Everyone loves this hearty recipe, especially when it's spooned over mashed potatoes...scrumptious!

2 to 3 lbs. chicken
2 10-3/4 oz. cans cream of
　chicken soup
8-oz. can sliced mushrooms,
　drained

1 c. chicken broth
1.35-oz. pkg. onion soup mix

Arrange chicken pieces in a slow cooker. Combine remaining ingredients; pour over chicken. Cover and cook on low setting for 5 to 6 hours. Serves 5.

Mashed potatoes are the perfect partner for creamy comfort foods. Make 'em in a jiffy! Quarter potatoes (no peeling required!) and cook in boiling water until tender, 10 to 20 minutes. Drain, mash right in the pot and stir in butter and a little milk to desired consistency.

Farmgirl Chicken & Dumplings

Vickie Chisom
Hardy, VA

This recipe was passed down from a special family member.
Add more vegetables if you like a thicker stew.

1 lb. boneless, skinless chicken
  breasts, cubed
16-oz. pkg. frozen mixed
  vegetables
1 onion, diced

3 cups low-sodium chicken
  broth, divided
1-1/2 c. buttermilk biscuit
  baking mix

Combine chicken, vegetables and onion in a slow cooker. Set aside 1/2 cup plus one tablespoon broth; pour remaining broth into slow cooker. Cover and cook on high setting for 2 hours. Stir biscuit mix with reserved broth until moistened. Drop by tablespoonfuls over hot chicken and vegetables. Cover and cook on high setting for 10 minutes; uncover. Cook for an additional 20 minutes, until dumplings are done. Serves 4 to 6.

Dried herbs tend to lose their flavor when slow-cooked for hours, so be sure to stir them in near the end of cooking time.

Root Beer Pulled Pork BBQ

Jill Ball
Highland, UT

This is a super Sunday recipe...pop it in the slow cooker and forget about it until dinnertime! Serve on crusty buns with a Carolina-style mustard BBQ sauce and all the trimmings...dill pickle spears, thinly sliced raw onion, pickled Italian banana peppers and a side of crisp homemade coleslaw. It's the best!

2 onions, sliced and divided
2 T. garlic, minced
4-lb. pork roast
1/2 t. salt
1/2 t. pepper
4-1/2 c. root beer, divided
16-oz. bottle favorite barbecue
  or chili sauce

Place one sliced onion in the bottom of a slow cooker; add garlic. Sprinkle roast with salt and pepper; place in slow cooker. Add 1-1/2 cups root beer to slow cooker. Cover and cook on low setting for 8 to 10 hours, or on high setting for 5 hours. Remove roast and set aside to cool. Discard onion and liquid in slow cooker. In a saucepan, bring sauce and remaining root beer to a boil; simmer for 30 minutes. When roast is cool enough to handle, shred with a fork, discarding bone and fat; return shredded meat to slow cooker. Stir in sauce mixture and remaining onion. Cover and cook on high setting for one to 3 hours, until onion is soft. Serves 12.

Monday burger night, Wednesday spaghetti night, Saturday slow-cooker night... dinner traditions make meal planning a snap and give everyone something to look forward to. Why not start a few of your own, featuring your family's favorite simple-to-fix foods?

14

Pulled Beef Sandwiches

Melinda Hokoth
Rockford, IL

Serve this tender beef spooned onto toasted hoagie rolls,
topped with slices of mozzarella cheese...delicious!

2-lb. beef chuck roast
garlic powder, salt and pepper to
    taste
1/2 t. meat tenderizer

1 c. beef broth
1-1/4 c. water
1.35-oz. pkg. onion soup mix

Sprinkle roast with seasonings and tenderizer; place in a slow cooker.
Pour in broth and water. Cover and cook on low setting for 8 to
10 hours. When roast is very tender, shred with 2 forks. Stir in soup
mix and continue cooking for 30 minutes. Makes 4 to 6 servings.

Shredded beef, pork or chicken sandwiches are oh-so easy to fix
and a real crowd-pleaser! Serve them on busy family nights
or tote them to potlucks right in the slow cooker.

No-Peek Shepherd's Pie

Melanie Lowe
Dover, DE

*We love this filling one-dish meal! Sometimes I'll use ground beef
instead of sausage...it's good either way. Just add some
brown & serve rolls and dinner is served.*

1 lb. ground pork sausage,
  browned and drained
10-oz. pkg. frozen peas
  and carrots

24-oz. pkg. prepared mashed
  potatoes
12-oz. jar beef gravy

Combine sausage with peas and carrots in a slow cooker. Spoon
mashed potatoes evenly over mixture; top with gravy. Do not stir.
Cover and cook on low setting for 4 to 6 hours. Makes 6 servings.

Make some pretty bookmarks to mark favorite go-to dinner
recipes in all your cookbooks...it's easy! Cut scrapbooking paper
into wide strips with decorative-edge scissors, punch a hole
at the top and add a narrow ribbon.

"Rotisserie" Roast Chicken

Mary Ann Lewis
Olive Branch, MS

You'll love this easy way to make a Sunday-best roast chicken!

5-lb. roasting chicken   seasoning salt to taste

Coat chicken with non-stick vegetable spray. Sprinkle seasoning salt over chicken and set aside. Tear off a 12-inch piece of aluminum foil and crumple into a ball; repeat to make a total of 8 foil balls. Arrange balls in the bottom of an oval slow cooker that has been coated with non-stick vegetable spray. Place chicken on top of foil balls; do not add any water. Cover and cook on low setting for 8 hours, or on high setting for 4 to 5 hours. Serves 8.

Save time with double-duty slow-cooker recipes by saving half for another meal. Use extra roast chicken as the start of a yummy noodle casserole, simmer shredded beef roast with barbecue sauce to serve in crusty buns...even spoon extra chili over hot dogs or into taco salads. The only limit is your imagination!

Kona Honey Chicken

Rogene Rogers
Bemidji, MN

*A family favorite! To complete the tropical theme, stir some
pineapple tidbits into your favorite creamy coleslaw.*

3 lbs. chicken
1/2 c. green onions, chopped
1/2 c. soy sauce

1/4 c. white wine or apple juice
1/2 c. water
1/2 c. honey

Place chicken pieces in a slow cooker. Mix together onions, sauce,
wine or juice and water; pour over chicken. Cover and cook on low
setting for 3 to 5 hours, until chicken is tender. Remove chicken from
slow cooker. Brush with honey and place on an ungreased broiler
pan. Broil for a few minutes until golden, brushing with honey several
times. Serve chicken with sauce from slow cooker. Serves 8 to 10.

Here's how to check whether a slow cooker is heating to the right
temperature. Pour 8 cups of water into the crock, cover and heat
on low setting for 8 hours. Uncover and immediately check the
water temperature with an instant-read kitchen thermometer. If
the slow cooker is working properly, it will read 185 degrees.

Autumn Apple Pork Roast

Vickie

*Add a side of sauerkraut and some creamy mashed potatoes...
a perfect meal for those cool fall days!*

4-lb. pork loin roast
salt and pepper to taste
6 tart apples, cored and
   quartered

1/4 c. apple juice
3 T. brown sugar, packed
1 t. ground ginger

Rub roast with salt and pepper. Brown roast under a broiler to remove
excess fat; drain. Place apples in the bottom of a slow cooker. Place
roast on top of apples. Mix together remaining ingredients and spoon
over roast. Cover and cook on low setting for 8 to 10 hours. Makes
6 to 8 servings.

Planning a festive holiday dinner? Let your slow cooker help out
by cooking up a scrumptious roast, or free up oven space by
preparing a savory slow-cooked side dish. Slow cookers are
so handy, you may want more than one!

Saucy Onion-Mushroom Beef

Jennifer Snyder
Myerstown, PA

This recipe is perfect for my family's busy life. Everyone likes it too, which can be a challenge in our household! I can serve this once a week and there are never any leftovers.

1-oz. pkg. onion-mushroom soup mix	1 c. cold water, divided
1/3 c. catsup	2 to 3-lb. beef chuck roast
1 T. Worcestershire sauce	2 T. cornstarch

Blend soup mix, catsup, sauce and 3/4 cup water; add 1/4 of mixture to a slow cooker. Place roast into slow cooker and pour remainder of mixture over top. Cover and cook on low setting for 6 to 8 hours, turning roast over halfway through cooking time. Combine cornstarch with remaining water; stir until cornstarch is dissolved. Add cornstarch mixture to slow cooker and stir until sauce thickens. Serves 4.

Fresh flowers on the dinner table are so cheerful...they don't need to be fancy. A simple bouquet of daisies, black-eyed Susans, cosmos and asters in a Mason jar is charming and takes only an instant to assemble.

Italian Beef Hoagies

Michelle Riley
Barnhart, MO

*We like to spread garlic butter on warm, toasted hoagie rolls
before adding the beef...scrumptious!*

3 to 4-lb. beef chuck roast
2 .6-oz. pkgs. zesty Italian
   salad dressing mix
2 c. water
24-oz. jar pepperoncinis,
   drained and liquid reserved

15 to 18 hoagie rolls, toasted
   and split
Garnish: shredded provolone
   cheese

Slice roast across the grain into 4 pieces and trim any fat. Place in
bottom of a slow cooker. Mix together dressing mix and water; pour
over beef. Cover and cook on low setting for 8 to 10 hours, until
tender; use forks to shred beef in slow cooker. Slice pepperoncinis
into rings and add to slow cooker along with reserved liquid from jar.
Cover and cook for a few more minutes, until heated through. Serve
beef on toasted rolls, topped with cheese. Serves 15 to 18.

Dinner and a movie! Just for fun, start family movie nights
with a favorite meal tie-in. Italian beef would be perfect
for *Rocky*, or how about down-home chicken & dumplings
and *The Wizard of Oz*? You're sure to think of lots of others.

Chicken Stroganoff

Cathy Hillier
Salt Lake City, UT

This easy recipe is delectable served over egg noodles. My family doesn't care for mushrooms, but if yours does, be sure to add some.

4 boneless, skinless chicken breasts, cubed
2 T. margarine, diced
.7-oz. pkg. Italian salad dressing mix

10-3/4 oz. can cream of chicken soup
8-oz. pkg. cream cheese, cubed

Place chicken, margarine and dressing mix in a slow cooker; toss to mix well. Cover and cook on low setting for 5 to 6 hours. Stir in soup and cream cheese. Cover; turn setting to high and cook for 30 minutes, until heated through. Serves 4.

Attach vintage porcelain or glass knobs in a row across a length of wood...just right for keeping tea towels and potholders handy.

Busy-Day Cheesy Chicken

Tiffany Brinkley
Broomfield, CO

My kids always look forward to this dish for dinner. Sometimes I spice things up a bit by using nacho cheese soup instead.

6 boneless, skinless chicken
   breasts
2 10-3/4 oz. cans Cheddar
   cheese soup

1/2 c. milk
1 t. garlic powder
salt and pepper to taste

Arrange chicken breasts in a slow cooker. Blend soup and milk in a bowl; pour mixture over chicken. Add seasonings. Cover and cook on high setting for about 6 hours, until chicken is tender. Makes 6 servings.

Give the slow-cooker crock a spritz of non-stick vegetable spray
before filling with dinner ingredients. Afterwards,
it will clean up in a jiffy!

Carol's Cheesy Potato Bake

Carol Fourman
Greenville, OH

I make this dish for every carry-in at church...if I bring something else,
everyone wants to know where the cheesy potatoes are!
It's so easy to make that I don't mind at all.

32-oz. pkg. frozen French fries
2 10-3/4 oz. cans cream of
  chicken soup

1 lb. smoked pork sausage, cut
  into bite-size pieces
2 c. shredded Cheddar cheese

Spray a slow cooker with non-stick vegetable spray. Layer ingredients
in the following order: half of French fries, one can of soup, half of
sausage and half of cheese. Repeat layers. Cover and cook on high
setting for 4 hours. Stir just before serving. Makes 10 to 12 servings.

Homemade buttermilk dressing is wonderful on salads...it's a
kid-friendly dip for raw veggies too! Blend 1/2 cup mayonnaise,
1/2 cup buttermilk, one teaspoon dried parsley, 1/2 teaspoon onion
powder, 1/4 teaspoon garlic powder, 1/8 teaspoon dill weed and a
little salt and pepper. Keep refrigerated.

Just 5 Ingredients!

Italian Sausages & Peppers

Geneva Rogers
Gillette, WY

A super-easy version of our favorite county fair food!
Spoon onto crusty rolls for a meal everyone will love.

2 lbs. Italian sausage links
1 green pepper, sliced into strips
1 onion, sliced and separated
   into rings

26-oz. jar spaghetti sauce

Layer sausages, pepper and onion in a slow cooker. Pour in sauce;
stir to coat ingredients well. Cover and cook on low setting for
6 hours. Serves 6.

Whip up some fruit smoothies for a healthy treat...they're
especially delectable with summer-ripe peaches, berries
and bananas! In a blender, combine 2 cups of fruit with
a cup of vanilla yogurt, a cup of ice cubes and a tablespoon
of honey. Blend until smooth, pour into tall glasses and enjoy.

Charlene's Chili Steak

Charlene Roberson
Weatherford, TX

When I was following a diet plan years ago, one of the requirements was to eat lots of meat, so I developed this recipe to make that easier. This is scrumptious served with mashed potatoes to hold all the tasty gravy...although the mashed potatoes weren't on the diet plan!

1 c. cocktail vegetable juice
1 c. water
1 T. chili powder

1-1/2 to 2 lbs. beef round steak, sliced into serving-size pieces
1 onion, sliced 1/2-inch thick

Combine juice and water; pour into a slow cooker set to high setting. When mixture bubbles and starts to steam, sprinkle in chili powder and stir slightly. Carefully add steak pieces to the hot liquid. Cover and cook on low setting for 6 to 8 hours, or on high setting for 3 to 4 hours. About one hour before serving, place onion on top of the steak pieces. Cover and cook for one additional hour. Serves 4.

Slow cookers are a super budget helper! Cheaper cuts of beef like round steak and chuck roast cook up fork-tender, juicy and flavorful...there's simply no need to purchase more expensive cuts.

Georgia Tomato Roast

Denise Jones
Fountain, FL

Every year, my husband picks tomatoes in the U-Pick fields of his Georgia hometown and brings home lots for us to eat, can, freeze and give away. I came up with this very delicious idea to use up all those home-canned tomatoes.

4 to 5-lb. beef chuck roast
14-1/2 oz. can plain or Italian-
   style stewed tomatoes
1 onion, cut into chunks

1 green pepper, cut into chunks
1 to 2 cloves garlic, quartered
salt and pepper to taste
Optional: 1/4 to 1/2 c. water

Layer roast, tomatoes with juice and remaining ingredients except water in a slow cooker. Add a little water if roast is very lean. Cover and cook on low setting for about 6 hours, until roast is tender. Serves 4 to 6.

Browning meat before slow cooking adds flavor and color.
If you wish, toss meat with a little flour and brown in oil. It isn't
really necessary, though! The exception is ground meat...
browning eliminates excess fat.

Company Chicken Dijon

Kay Marone
Des Moines, IA

*Just toss the ingredients in the slow cooker in the morning,
then arrive home to a delicious dinner. Serve with cooked rice
and steamed, buttered broccoli spears...mmm!*

4 to 6 boneless, skinless
   chicken breasts
10-3/4 oz. can cream of
   mushroom soup

2 T. Dijon mustard
2 T. water
2 t. cornstarch
1/8 t. pepper

Place chicken breasts in a slow cooker. Combine remaining ingredients
and spoon over chicken. Cover and cook on low setting for 6 to
8 hours. Makes 4 to 6 servings.

A casual potluck supper is perfect for catching up with
family & friends. Everyone is sure to discover new favorites,
so be sure to have each person bring along extra copies
of their recipe to share.

Zesty Chicken Barbecue

Tara Horton
Gooseberry Patch

This recipe is a staple at our house...we all love it! There are so many tasty varieties of bottled barbecue sauce on the market that I can easily change it up by using a different flavor.

6 boneless, skinless chicken
   breasts
1-1/2 c. barbecue sauce
1/2 c. zesty Italian salad
   dressing

1/4 c. brown sugar, packed
2 T. Worcestershire sauce

Arrange chicken breasts in a slow cooker. Blend together remaining ingredients and pour over chicken. Cover and cook on low setting for 6 to 8 hours. Serves 6.

Canning jars can often be picked up for a song at tag sales.
Use them as country-style tumblers to serve icy cold lemonade
or apple cider...how refreshing!

Judy's Easy Meatloaf

Judy Williams
Oil Springs, KY

This slow-cooker meatloaf is great for busy cooks! It's easy to adjust the seasonings to your family's preference. Try using hot pork sausage if you enjoy spicy flavors.

2 to 3 lbs. ground beef
1 lb. ground pork sausage
1-1/2 c. long-cooking oats,
　uncooked
2 eggs, beaten
3/4 c. evaporated milk

1 onion, chopped
6 T. sugar
2 T. chili powder
1 t. salt
1/2 t. pepper
14-1/2 oz. can diced tomatoes

Combine all ingredients except tomatoes and mix well. Shape into a loaf; place in an oval slow cooker. Cover with tomatoes. Cover and cook on low setting for 6 to 8 hours, or 2 to 4 hours on high setting. Serves 8 to 10.

Give family dinner conversations a little boost.
Write down whimsical questions like "If you could live anywhere in the world, where would you choose?" and "What storybook character would you like to be?" Fill a jar with questions, then have everyone take turns pulling out and answering questions. The answers are sure to be fun!

Slow-Cooked Mac & Cheese

Mary Alice Veal
Mars Hill, NC

This tastes just like the old-fashioned macaroni & cheese that Grandma used to make. It is delicious and oh-so easy!

8-oz. pkg. elbow macaroni,
  cooked
2 eggs, beaten
12-oz. can evaporated milk
1-1/2 c. milk

3 c. shredded sharp Cheddar
  cheese
1/2 c. margarine, melted
1 t. salt
pepper to taste

Mix all ingredients together and pour into a lightly greased slow cooker. Cover and cook on low setting for 3 to 4 hours. Makes 6 to 8 servings.

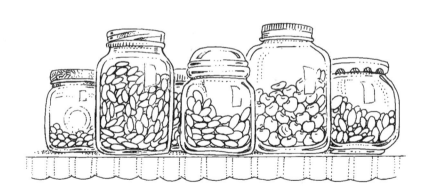

Oversized clear glass jars make attractive canisters for storing macaroni, dried beans and rice. Because the contents are visible, you'll always know when it's time to restock.

Creamy Chicken Sandwiches

Trisha Melvin
McGuire AFB, NJ

*In Ohio, where I used to live, these delicious sandwiches are
a tradition at ball games, potlucks and county fairs!*

1 lb. boneless, skinless chicken
  breasts
10-3/4 oz. can cream of chicken
  soup
14-1/2 oz. can chicken broth

1/8 t. salt
1/8 t. pepper
Optional: 6 to 8 saltine crackers,
  crushed
6 sandwich buns, split

Put chicken in the bottom of a slow cooker; add soup and broth.
Cover and cook on low setting for 8 to 9 hours, until chicken is tender
and mixture is thickened. If too thin, stir in a few crushed crackers
to thicken. Shred chicken with a fork and serve on buns. Makes
6 sandwiches.

For best results when cooking in a slow cooker, be sure the crock
is filled at least half full and no more than two-thirds full.

Mom's Mini Reubens

Cheryl Breeden
North Platte, NE

This was always my mom's favorite recipe during football season.
It's so yummy, easy and fun for guests to fix their own sandwiches...
even if our team lost, dinner was always a winner!

2 16-oz. pkgs. shredded Swiss
   cheese
8-oz. bottle Thousand Island
   salad dressing
32-oz. pkg. refrigerated
   sauerkraut, drained and
   chopped

1/4 to 1/2 lb. deli corned beef,
   chopped
Optional: 1 t. caraway seed
1 to 2 loaves party rye
Garnish: dill pickle slices

Put all ingredients except party rye and pickles in a slow cooker. Cover and cook on low setting for about 4 hours, or until mixture is hot and cheese is melted. Stir to blend well. To serve, arrange party rye slices and pickles on separate plates around slow cooker. Makes 10 to 12 servings.

Mini versions of favorite hot sandwiches are oh-so appealing on party platters...they help food go farther too! Try using small sandwich rolls or brown & serve dinner rolls instead of full-size buns.

Cranberry Pork Chops

Jill Ball
Highland, UT

One of our favorite meals! So easy to prepare, but it looks and tastes likes you put a lot of time into it. I first tried it during the holiday season, and my family loved it so much that I now serve it several times a year.

6 pork chops
1/2 t. salt
pepper to taste
16-oz. can jellied cranberry
    sauce
1/2 c. cranberry juice cocktail
    or apple juice

1/4 c. sugar
2 T. spicy mustard
1/4 c. cold water
2 T. cornstarch

Season pork chops with salt and pepper; place in a slow cooker. Combine cranberry sauce, juice, sugar and mustard in a bowl; pour over pork chops. Cover and cook for 6 to 8 hours on high setting. Shortly before serving time, remove pork chops to a platter; keep warm. Combine cold water and cornstarch in a saucepan. Cook over medium heat, stirring continuously, until mixture becomes thick. Add liquid from slow cooker to saucepan and boil until thickened. Serve pork chops with sauce. Makes 6 servings.

Good sound cooking
makes a contented home.

~Georges-Auguste Escoffier

Slow-Cooker Baked Apples

Eva Jo Hoyle
Mexico, MO

Delectable as either a side or a dessert! Sometimes I'll even fill the slow cooker late at night so we can enjoy them for breakfast.

8 Jonathan or Granny Smith
   apples, cored
1/3 c. raisins
1/3 c. chopped nuts
1/3 c. brown sugar, packed

1-1/2 t. apple pie spice
2 T. margarine, sliced
1/2 c. apple cider
1 T. lemon juice

Remove peel from top 1/3 of apples. Mix raisins, nuts and brown sugar; spoon into apples. Arrange apples in a greased slow cooker. Sprinkle with spice; dot with margarine. Mix cider and lemon juice and drizzle over apples. Cover and cook on low setting for 8 hours. Serves 8.

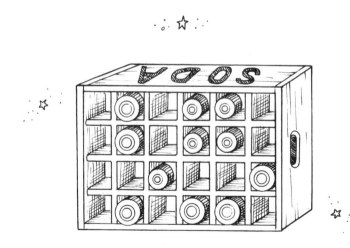

A vintage wooden soda crate makes a handy spice rack... enjoy it just as it is, or freshen it up with a coat of bright paint.

Chicken Sausage & Pasta

JoAnn

While on vacation, we tried this dish at an Italian restaurant and loved it. I was really pleased with how well it turned out in a slow cooker...now we can enjoy it often!

1/2 c. yellow onion, minced
1 clove garlic, minced
1 T. olive oil
1 lb. sweet Italian chicken sausage links, removed from casings and chopped
28-oz. can stewed tomatoes, drained

1-1/2 c. red or yellow pepper, sliced
3/4 c. fresh basil, chopped
red pepper flakes, salt and pepper to taste
cooked rotini pasta

In a skillet over medium heat, cook onion and garlic in oil until translucent. Add sausage to skillet; cook for several minutes, just until beginning to brown. Drain; transfer skillet mixture to a slow cooker. Add remaining ingredients except pasta; stir to blend. Cover and cook on high setting for 2-1/2 to 3 hours, until peppers are tender. Serve over cooked pasta. Makes 4 servings.

A whimsical centerpiece for an Italian dinner! Take a handful of long pasta like spaghetti, bucatini or curly strands of fusilli and fan it out in a wide-mouthed vase.

Easy Meatballs in Sauce

Connie Bryant
Topeka, KS

Spoon these yummy meatballs into crusty hard rolls or serve over pasta. Pass the Parmesan cheese, please!

1-1/2 lbs. ground beef
1-1/4 c. Italian-seasoned dry
  bread crumbs
1/4 c. fresh parsley, chopped
2 cloves garlic, minced

1 onion, chopped
1 egg, beaten
28-oz. jar spaghetti sauce
16-oz. can crushed tomatoes
14-1/4 oz. can tomato purée

In a large bowl, combine all ingredients except spaghetti sauce, tomatoes and tomato purée. Mix by hand and form into 16 meatballs; set aside. In a slow cooker, stir together remaining ingredients. Add meatballs to sauce mixture and turn to coat. Cover and cook on low setting for 6 to 8 hours. Makes 4 servings.

Vintage tin picnic baskets make roomy storage for cookbooks, cookie cutters and all kinds of other kitchen items.

Kay's Sticky Chicken

Karen Hazelett
Fremont, IN

This recipe is delicious and incredibly easy...make it the night before, pop it in the slow cooker and forget about it all day! It's one of my husband's favorite meals. I received this recipe from my good friend, Kay, and have shared it many times with co-workers.

3 to 5-lb. roasting chicken
4 t. salt
2 t. paprika
1 t. cayenne pepper
1 t. onion powder

1 t. dried thyme
1 t. white pepper
1/2 t. garlic powder
1/2 t. pepper
1 onion, halved

Pat chicken dry with paper towels. Combine salt and spices in a small bowl. Rub mixture evenly onto chicken, both inside and out, making sure to rub deep into the skin. Insert onion halves into chicken. Place chicken in a large plastic zipping bag; seal and refrigerate overnight. In the morning, remove chicken from bag and place in a slow cooker. Do not add any water. Cover and cook on low setting for 8 to 10 hours. Makes 6 to 8 servings.

Set out a basket of rolled-up washcloths, moistened with lemon-scented water and warmed briefly in the microwave. Sure to be appreciated when yummy-but-messy foods like barbecued ribs and fried chicken are on the menu!

Creole Beef & Noodles

Kerry Mayer
Dunham Springs, LA

This dish tastes like it took a lot of effort, but stirs up in a jiffy!
The night before, I move the beef from the freezer into the fridge. In the
morning, it slices easily while still partly frozen.

3/4 lb. beef round steak, sliced
    into thin strips
1 green pepper, chopped
1 onion, chopped
1 tomato, chopped
1 clove garlic, pressed
1 t. dried parsley

1/2 t. salt
1/8 t. pepper
1 cube beef bouillon
1/2 c. boiling water
2 T. cornstarch
2 T. cold water
cooked wide egg noodles

Combine beef, vegetables, garlic and seasonings in a slow cooker. Dissolve bouillon cube in boiling water; add to slow cooker. Cover and cook on low setting for 7 to 8 hours, until beef is tender. Shortly before serving time, dissolve cornstarch in cold water; stir into slow cooker. Turn to high setting. Cover and cook for about 10 minutes, until slightly thickened. To serve, spoon beef mixture over cooked noodles. Makes 3 to 4 servings.

Vintage magazine recipe ads make fun wall art for the kitchen when framed. They're easy to find at flea markets...look for ones featuring shimmery gelatin salads, golden mac & cheese or other favorites like Mom used to make!

Mushroom Burgers

John Alexander
New Britain, CT

Serve on onion buns or atop egg noodles...delicious!

2 lbs. ground beef
1 egg, beaten
1 c. onion, finely chopped
1/2 c. shredded Cheddar cheese
2 T. catsup
2 T. evaporated milk

1/2 c. saltine cracker crumbs
salt and pepper to taste
1/2 c. all-purpose flour
1 to 2 T. oil
10-3/4 oz. can cream of
  mushroom soup

Combine beef, egg, onion, cheese, catsup, milk, cracker crumbs, salt and pepper in a large bowl. Mix well and form into 8 patties; roll in flour. In a skillet over medium-high heat, brown patties in oil; drain. Layer patties in a slow cooker with spoonfuls of soup. Cover and cook on high setting for 3 to 4 hours. Serves 8.

Start a tradition of having a regular night for dinner guests. Many slow-cooker recipes make plenty of food for sharing. Invite a neighbor or co-worker you've wanted to get to know better... encourage your kids to invite a friend. You'll be so glad you did!

Chris's Chuck Wagon Beans

Christina Mendoza
Alamogordo, NM

You can cut down on chopping time by using half of a one-pound package of frozen mixed-color pepper strips. Add a pan of your favorite warm cornbread for a hearty, satisfying meal.

16-oz. pkg. dried navy or
   pinto beans
6 c. water
1 lb. ground beef
1 onion, chopped
1 clove garlic, minced

1 green or red pepper, chopped
8-oz. can tomato sauce
1/2 t. dried oregano
1/4 t. cayenne pepper, or to
   taste
salt to taste

Place beans in a large kettle; cover with water. Bring to a boil; cover and cook for 2 minutes. Remove from heat; cover and let stand for one hour. Drain beans in a colander. Add beans and 6 cups water to a slow cooker; set aside. Brown ground beef in a skillet along with onion, garlic and green or red pepper; drain. Remove beef mixture to slow cooker with a slotted spoon. Stir in remaining ingredients; add more water if necessary to bring liquid level above beans. Cover and cook on high setting for 6 hours, or on low setting for 10 hours, until beans are tender. Makes 6 to 8 servings.

A western theme is fun and easy for casual get-togethers. Set the table with pie plates, Mason jar tumblers and bandanna napkins. Serve up grilled burgers and fixin's, baked beans and tortilla chips with salsa. Fruit cobbler baked in a Dutch oven will round out a memorable occasion.

Sweet & Saucy Spareribs

Susie Backus
Gooseberry Patch

*These scrumptious ribs are equally at home at a summer picnic
or at a lucky New Year's Day dinner.*

2 lbs. pork spareribs, sliced into
   serving-size portions
10-3/4 oz. can tomato soup
1 onion, chopped
3 cloves garlic, minced

1 T. brown sugar, packed
1 T. Worcestershire sauce
2 T. soy sauce
1/4 c. cold water
1 t. cornstarch

Place ribs in a stockpot and add water to cover. Bring to a boil; reduce heat and simmer for 15 minutes. Drain; arrange ribs in a slow cooker. Mix together remaining ingredients except cold water and cornstarch; pour over ribs. Cover and cook on low setting for 6 to 8 hours. When ribs are tender, place them on a serving platter; cover to keep warm. Pour sauce from slow cooker into a saucepan over medium-high heat. Stir together cold water and cornstarch; stir into sauce and bring to a boil. Cook and stir until sauce has reached desired thickness. Serve ribs with sauce. Makes 4 servings.

Slow-cook a pot of creamy beans to serve with pork. Rinse and drain 1/2 pound dried navy beans. Place them in a slow cooker and stir in a chopped onion, a tablespoon of bacon drippings or butter and 5 cups boiling water. Cover and cook on high for 4 hours, stirring occasionally. Don't add salt until the beans are tender. So easy!

Asian Country-Style Ribs

Melody Taynor
Everett, WA

For a super-easy side, steam a package of frozen stir-fry veggies...
top with crunchy chow mein noodles. Dinner is served!

4 lbs. boneless country-style
  pork ribs
1/4 c. brown sugar, packed
1 c. soy sauce
1/4 c. sesame oil
2 T. olive oil
2 T. rice vinegar

2 T. lime juice
2 T. garlic, minced
2 T. fresh ginger, peeled and
  grated
1 t. hot pepper sauce
cooked rice

Place ribs in a large plastic zipping bag. Stir together remaining
ingredients except rice; pour over ribs. Seal bag and refrigerate for
8 hours to overnight, turning bag occasionally to coat ribs with
marinade. Drain marinade and discard; place ribs in a slow cooker.
Cover and cook on low setting for 8 to 9 hours, until tender. Drain;
shred ribs using 2 forks. Serve over cooked rice. Serves 6.

Savor ripe summer fruit by heaping a hollowed-out watermelon
half with melon balls, juicy strawberries, sliced nectarines and
kiwi fruit. Drizzle with a little honey and orange juice...delectable!

Chicken Cordon Bleu

Beth Kramer
Port Saint Lucie, FL

*I always used to fix this dish in the oven when we lived up north.
When we moved to Florida, I was really glad to find a slow-cooker
version so I didn't have to heat up the kitchen!*

4 to 6 boneless, skinless
   chicken breasts
4 to 6 slices deli ham
4 to 6 slices Swiss cheese

10-3/4 oz. can cream of
   mushroom soup
1/4 c. milk
cooked egg noodles

Place each chicken breast between 2 pieces of wax paper; flatten with
a meat mallet. Top with a slice of ham and a slice of cheese. Roll up
and secure with wooden toothpicks. Arrange chicken rolls in a slow
cooker, making 2 layers if necessary. Blend soup and milk; pour over
chicken. Cover and cook on low setting for 4 hours, or until chicken
juices run clear. Serve chicken rolls over noodles; top with sauce from
slow cooker. Serves 4 to 6.

Mix up some zesty oil & vinegar salad dressing. Combine 3/4 cup
olive oil, 1/4 cup white wine vinegar, 3/4 teaspoon salt and
1/4 teaspoon pepper in a small jar. Add some minced garlic,
if you like. Screw on the lid and shake well. Keep refrigerated.

Slow-Cooker Sage Stuffing

Brenna Carey
Shickshinny, PA

I use this recipe every Thanksgiving because it's so delicious...
it frees up space in the oven too.

14 c. bread cubes
3 c. celery, chopped
1-1/2 c. onion, chopped
1-1/2 t. to 1 T. dried sage

1 t. salt
1/2 t. pepper
1-1/4 c. butter, melted

In a very large bowl, combine all ingredients except butter; mix well. Add butter and toss. Spoon into a lightly greased slow cooker. Cover and cook on low setting 4 to 5 hours. Makes 8 to 10 servings.

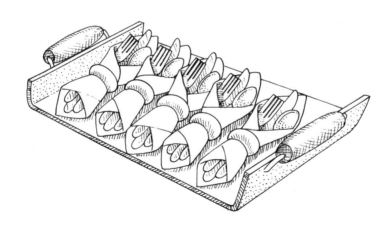

For a dinner party or holiday buffet, roll up sets of flatware in table napkins and place in a shallow tray. An easy do-ahead for the hostess...guests will find it simple to pull out individual sets too.

Beefy Macaroni & Cheese

Shelley Turner
Boise, ID

So hearty, warm and filling...perfect comfort food!

1-1/2 lbs. ground beef
1 onion, chopped
10-3/4 oz. can cream of
    mushroom or chicken soup
15-oz. can stewed tomatoes
1-1/2 oz. pkg. cheese sauce mix

1/4 c. water
2 T. tomato paste
1 c. shredded Cheddar cheese
8-oz. pkg. elbow macaroni,
    cooked

Brown ground beef and onion together in a skillet over medium heat; drain. Combine beef mixture with remaining ingredients except cheese and macaroni in a slow cooker. Cover and cook on low setting for 6 hours. About 30 minutes before serving, stir in cheese and cooked macaroni. Cover and continue cooking for an additional 15 to 30 minutes, until heated through and cheese is melted. Stir before serving. Serves 4.

Frozen leftovers from a slow-cooked meal make great quick lunches and dinners. Thaw and reheat them using the microwave, stovetop or oven...slow cookers don't work well for reheating frozen foods.

Grandma's Beef Casserole

Eva Jo Hoyle
Mexico, MO

My grandmother would put this recipe in the slow cooker on fall Saturdays when we were raking leaves or picking apples at the orchard. It always smelled so good when we came inside!

2 lbs. stew beef, cubed
1/4 c. all-purpose flour
10-3/4 oz. can cream of
   mushroom soup
1.35-oz. pkg. onion soup mix

4-oz. can whole mushrooms,
   drained
1/2 c. red wine or beef broth
12-oz. pkg. medium egg
   noodles, cooked

Put beef cubes in a plastic zipping bag. Add flour; seal bag and shake to coat well. Brown beef in a heavy skillet that has been sprayed with non-stick vegetable spray; drain. In a slow cooker, combine beef with remaining ingredients except noodles. Cover and cook on low setting for 8 to 10 hours, or on high setting for 5 to 6 hours. To serve, spoon over cooked noodles. Serves 6.

Keep a shaker canister of quick-mixing flour on hand for dusting pork chops, cubes of stew beef or other meat before browning.

Sausage & Peppers Sauce

Joyce Hallisey
Mount Gilead, NC

A friend recently shared with me how she prepares Italian sausages and peppers in the slow cooker. I made some of my own additions to transform it into a delicious sauce that I could serve over pasta.

1 lb. sweet Italian pork
   sausages, sliced into thirds
1 T. oil
1 green pepper, chopped
1 onion, diced

1 t. garlic, minced
1 t. dried basil
14-1/2 oz. can petite diced
   tomatoes, divided
cooked thin spaghetti

In a skillet over medium-high heat, brown sausage in oil on all sides. Reduce heat and simmer for about 10 minutes; drain sausage and set aside. To same skillet, add pepper, onion and garlic; stir-fry until tender. Stir in basil. Spoon 1/4 of undrained tomatoes into a slow cooker. Add sausage, another 1/4 of tomatoes, pepper mixture and remaining tomatoes on top. Cover and cook on high setting for one hour. Reduce to low setting and cook for 3 to 4 hours, stirring occasionally, until sausage is tender. Serve spooned over cooked spaghetti. Serves 4.

Bake bread in your slow cooker! Rub butter generously over a 9"x5" loaf pan and a frozen bread loaf. Set the pan in an oval slow cooker and add the loaf. Cover and cook on low setting until the dough thaws and begins to rise, 2 to 3 hours. Turn to high setting and continue cooking for another 2 to 3 hours, until the loaf is golden and sounds hollow when tapped. Yum!

Green Chile Flank Steak

Connie Hilty
Pearland, TX

So full of flavor...so easy to do!

1-1/2 lb. beef flank steak, halved	2 T. vinegar
1 T. oil	1-1/4 t. chili powder
1 onion, sliced	1 t. garlic powder
1/3 c. water	1/2 t. sugar
4-oz. can chopped green chiles	1/2 t. salt
	1/8 t. pepper

In a skillet over medium-high heat, brown beef in oil; transfer to a slow cooker. Add onion to skillet and sauté for one minute. Gradually add water to skillet, stirring to loosen browned bits. Add remaining ingredients and bring to a boil; pour over beef. Cover and cook on low setting for 7 to 8 hours. Slice beef on the diagonal; serve with onion and juices from slow cooker. Makes 4 to 6 servings.

Broiled roma tomatoes make a tasty, quick garnish for steak. Place tomato halves cut-side up on a broiler pan. Toss together equal amounts of Italian-seasoned dry bread crumbs and grated Parmesan cheese with a little oil. Spoon onto tomatoes and broil until golden.

Southwestern Creamy Chicken

Jami Rodolph
Lolo, MT

*One day I had a whole chicken in the fridge and decided to try
something new...this is what I came up with. It is a family favorite
now. This is a great dish to make when you're having company for
dinner, because it makes a lot and is really yummy!*

5-lb. roasting chicken	1 t. red pepper flakes
1 T. garlic, minced	2 c. water
1 T. chili powder	1-1/2 c. frozen corn
1 T. ground cumin	1 c. whipping cream or
1 T. salt	whole milk
1 T. dried cilantro	cooked rice
2 t. paprika	

Place chicken in a slow cooker. Mix garlic and seasonings; sprinkle
over chicken. Add water to slow cooker. Cover and cook on high
setting for about 4 hours, until chicken juices run clear. Remove
chicken from slow cooker to a platter, reserving broth; allow to cool
for about 30 minutes. Shred chicken, discarding skin and bones. Place
chicken in a large skillet. Measure reserved broth, adding water if
necessary to equal 4 to 5 cups; add to skillet along with frozen corn.
Bring to a simmer over medium heat; cook until corn is tender. Stir
in cream or milk and heat through. To serve, spoon over cooked rice.
Makes 8 servings.

*A clear plastic over-the-door shoe organizer is super for pantry
storage...just slip gravy mix packets, spice jars and other
small items into the pockets.*

Firehouse Chicken

Ronda Hauss
Louisville, KY

My stepfather, a former firefighter, taught me how to make this easy, delicious dish. It was a hit at the firehouse, too! The sauce is also wonderful over fresh-baked bread.

2 10-3/4 oz. cans cream
  of mushroom soup
14-1/2 oz. can chicken broth
6-oz. jar sliced mushrooms,
  drained

1.35-oz. pkg. onion soup mix
2 lbs. boneless, skinless chicken
  breasts, cubed if desired
cooked rice

Mix all ingredients except chicken and rice in a slow cooker until well combined. Add chicken; stir to coat. Cover and cook on low setting for 8 hours, or for 4 hours on high setting. To serve, spoon over cooked rice. Serves 4.

Stirring rice with a spoon while it's cooking will cause the grains to stick together. Instead, gently fluff the rice with a fork after cooking...it's sure to be fluffy every time!

Savory Spuds

Sherry Gordon
Arlington Heights, IL

Potluck-perfect and oh-so easy! Depending on what's in the cupboard, sometimes I'll use cream of chicken, mushroom or cheese soup. They're all tasty!

2 lbs. new potatoes, peeled
10-3/4 oz. can cream of
  celery soup
1/4 c. sour cream
2 T. water

2 T. green onions, chopped
2 cloves garlic, minced
1 t. dill weed
1/2 t. salt

Place potatoes in a lightly greased slow cooker. Mix together remaining ingredients and add to potatoes; stir well. Cover and cook on low setting for 5 to 6 hours. Makes 4 to 6 servings.

Cut slices of crunchy carrot, zucchini and radish into stars, flowers and other fun shapes with mini cookie cutters... kids will eat their veggies happily!

Country Corn Pudding

Angela Lively
Baxter, TN

*With four kinds of corn, this new twist on an old favorite
is sure to be scrumptious!*

16-oz. pkg. frozen corn
2 11-oz. cans sweet corn &
   diced peppers
14-3/4 oz. can creamed corn

6-1/2 oz. pkg. corn muffin mix
3/4 c. water
1/4 c. butter, melted
1 t. salt

Mix all ingredients well; pour into a slow cooker. Cover and cook on low setting for 5 to 6 hours, stirring after 3 hours. Makes 8 servings.

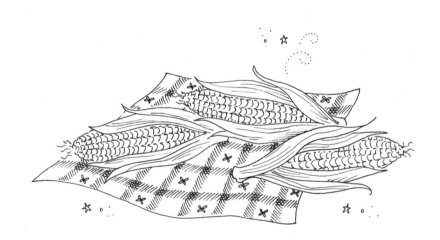

At the end of the week, turn leftovers into a buffet-style meal. Set out casserole portions in pretty dishes, toss veggies into a salad and add a basket of warm rolls. Arrange everything on a counter...everyone is sure to come looking for their favorites!

Beef Tips & Gravy

Susan Ice
Simpsonville, SC

The house smells sooo good when this is cooking...the tender beef just melts in your mouth. A real warmer-upper for chilly weather!

1 c. all-purpose flour
1 t. onion powder
1 t. garlic powder
salt and pepper to taste
2-1/2 lbs. beef tips or
   stew beef, cubed
2 to 3 T. oil

1 c. water
.87-oz. pkg. brown gravy mix
1/4 c. Worcestershire sauce
1/4 c. soy sauce
mashed potatoes or cooked
   egg noodles

Mix flour and seasonings in a large plastic zipping bag. Add beef; shake to coat beef thoroughly. Pour oil into a large heavy skillet and heat over medium-high heat for 2 to 3 minutes. Add beef to skillet; brown on all sides. Blend water, gravy mix and sauces in a slow cooker; add beef. Cover and cook on low setting for 6 to 8 hours, or on high setting for 4 to 5 hours. Add a little water if needed to thin gravy mixture. Serve over mashed potatoes or cooked noodles. Serves 4 to 6.

Create mini recipe cards listing the ingredients of favorite one-dish dinners. Glue a button magnet on the back and place on the fridge...so handy whenever it's time to make out a shopping list!

Mushroom Roast

Kelly Simpson-McLaughlin
Sioux Falls, SD

I've tried a lot of cooking "experiments"...this roast is easily my best success! Cooking the roast in good-quality beef broth instead of water really makes a difference in flavor.

3-1/2 to 4-1/2 lb. beef chuck
  roast
garlic salt, salt and pepper to
  taste
29-oz. container beef broth
1-oz. pkg. onion-mushroom
  soup mix

1 onion, diced
4 to 6 potatoes, peeled
  and sliced
2 10-3/4 oz. cans cream of
  mushroom soup
8-oz. pkg. sliced mushrooms
4 carrots, peeled and chopped

Sprinkle roast with seasonings to taste. Combine broth, soup mix, onion and potatoes in a large slow cooker; place roast on top. Pour soup over top of roast; add mushrooms. Cover and cook on low setting for 8 to 10 hours, or on high setting for 5 to 6 hours. Add carrots to slow cooker halfway through cook time. If liquid does not completely cover roast, turn every hour to keep roast moistened. Serves 6 to 8.

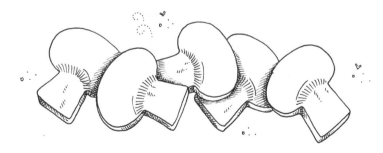

Slow-cooker gravy...it's a must with mashed potatoes! Remove the roast to a platter, leaving juices in the slow cooker. Make a smooth paste of 1/4 cup flour or cornstarch and 1/4 cup cold water. Pour into the slow cooker and stir well. Turn the cooker to the high setting and cook for 15 minutes once the mixture comes to a boil.

Turkey & Spinach Lasagna

Pamela Stump
Chino Hills, CA

Whenever I used no-boil lasagna noodles in casseroles, I never felt that they were cooked thoroughly. So I tried them in my slow cooker, thinking that it would be more moist...it worked!

1 lb. ground turkey
1 t. dried oregano
salt and pepper to taste
15-oz. container ricotta cheese
8-oz. pkg. shredded mozzarella
   cheese
10-oz. pkg. frozen spinach,
   cooked and drained

9-oz. pkg. no-boil lasagna
   noodles, uncooked and
   broken to fit
26-oz. jar spaghetti sauce
   with mushrooms
1/4 c. hot water

In a skillet over medium heat, brown turkey with seasonings; drain. Mix together cheeses and spinach. Layer as follows in a slow cooker: half of dry noodles, half of turkey, half of sauce and half of cheese mixture. Repeat layers in same order, ending with cheese. Pour hot water over all. Cover and cook on low setting for 4-1/2 hours. Let stand for a few minutes before serving. Serves 6 to 8.

Keep mini pots of your favorite fresh herbs like oregano, chives, parsley and basil on a sunny kitchen windowsill...they'll be right at your fingertips for any recipe!

Slow-Cooker Pepperoni Pizza

Kelly Alderson
Erie, PA

My kids can't get enough of this yummy pasta dish! Add sliced mushrooms, black olives and any other ingredients to make it just the way you like your pizza.

2 14-oz. jars pizza sauce
10-3/4 oz. can tomato soup
1-1/2 lbs. ground beef, browned
   and drained
8-oz. pkg. rigatoni pasta,
   cooked

16-oz. pkg. shredded
   mozzarella cheese
8-oz. pkg. sliced pepperoni

Mix together sauce and soup; set aside. Alternate layers in a slow cooker, using half each of beef, pasta, cheese, sauce mixture and pepperoni. Repeat layers. Cover and cook on low setting for 4 hours. Serves 6.

While waiting for a slow-cooked dinner, mix up some good clean fun with homemade bubble solution! Stir together 5 cups water, 2 cups dishwashing liquid and 1/2 cup light corn syrup. Let the kids explore the kitchen for pancake turners, strainers and other utensils to use as bubble wands.

Mexicali Beef & Beans

Virginia Watson
Scranton, PA

*Tasty and super-easy to put together! I like to mix oil & vinegar
salad dressing with salsa to top a lettuce and tomato salad.*

1 lb. ground beef
chili powder and garlic powder
  to taste
6 8-inch corn tortillas, torn
15-oz. can ranch-style beans
10-3/4 oz. can cream of
  mushroom soup

10-3/4 oz. can cream of chicken
  soup
14-1/2 oz. can diced tomatoes
  with green chiles
8-oz. pkg. pasteurized process
  cheese, cubed

Brown beef in a skillet over medium heat. Drain; add seasonings to
taste. Layer ingredients in a slow cooker, using half each of tortillas,
beans, soups, tomatoes, beef mixture and cheese. Repeat layers.
Cover and cook on low setting for 3 to 4 hours. Serves 4 to 6.

"Fried" ice cream is a yummy ending to a south-of-the-border
meal. Scoop balls of vanilla ice cream, roll them in crushed
sugar-coated corn flake cereal and return to the freezer.
At serving time, garnish with a drizzle of honey and
a dollop of whipped cream...scrumptious!

Ropa Vieja

Cheri Maxwell
Gulf Breeze, FL

The name of this traditional Cuban dish means...old clothes! It's descriptive of the way the beef shreds to "rags" when it's done. Spoon over a mixture of white rice and black beans, if you like.

1/2 c. pickled jalapeño peppers,
   drained and sliced
3 red or yellow peppers, sliced
1 onion, sliced
2 cloves garlic, sliced
1 t. ground cumin

1/2 t. dried oregano
1 bay leaf
1 t. salt
3 to 3-1/2 lbs. beef flank steak,
   cut into serving-size pieces
14-1/2 oz. can stewed tomatoes

Mix together jalapeños, peppers, onion, garlic and seasonings in a slow cooker. Top with beef. Pour tomatoes and juice over beef; do not stir. Cover and cook on low setting for 9 hours. Use a slotted spoon to transfer beef and vegetables to a large serving bowl. Reserve liquid; discard bay leaf. Shred beef with 2 forks. Stir liquid from slow cooker into beef mixture. Makes 4 to 6 servings.

Food is a wonderful way to learn about other places and cultures! Set the mood with background music...stop by the local library and pick up some Mexican, Caribbean or Italian music CDs.

Family Favorite Pot Roast

Nancy Hatton
Independence, MO

This recipe is always a hit! My kids called it "pull-apart meat" and it was always requested. You can add sliced onions, mushrooms or other veggies of your choice along with the potatoes and carrots.

3 to 4-lb. beef roast,
  2 to 4 inches thick
1 to 2 T. oil
4 to 5 potatoes, peeled
  and cubed
1 lb. baby carrots
5-oz. jar prepared horseradish

1-oz. pkg. onion soup mix
2 to 3 c. warm water
2 T. all-purpose flour or
  cornstarch
1/4 c. cold water
2 T. red steak sauce

In a large skillet over medium-high heat, brown roast on all sides in oil; drain. Add potatoes and carrots to a slow cooker; transfer roast to slow cooker. Spread horseradish thickly over top of roast; sprinkle with soup mix. Carefully pour in enough warm water around roast to come just to the top of roast. Cover and cook on high setting for 6 hours, until roast pulls apart very easily. Remove roast and vegetables to a serving platter and keep warm; reserve juices in slow cooker. Mix flour or cornstarch with cold water and add to juices in the slow cooker. Cook and stir on high setting until gravy reaches desired thickness, about 5 minutes. Stir steak sauce into gravy. Serves 6 to 8.

Slow-cooked beef chuck roast is always a winner! Any leftovers
will be equally delicious in sandwiches, soups or casseroles,
so be sure to choose a large roast even if your family is small.

Gammy's Chicken & Dressing

Melody Russell
Jackson, TN

A delicious made-from-scratch dinner that feeds a crowd! If you reserve the broth after simmering the chicken, use 1-3/4 cups of it in place of the canned broth. You may want to add a little more broth after layering, to moisten everything to your liking.

5 to 6 chicken breasts
5 c. cornbread, crumbled
2 c. biscuits, crumbled
2 eggs, beaten
1 onion, chopped
1 to 2 c. celery, chopped

1/2 c. butter, melted
1 t. to 1 T. dried sage
salt and pepper to taste
14-oz. can chicken broth
2 10-3/4 oz. cans cream of
   chicken soup, divided

Cover chicken with water in a large saucepan. Simmer over medium heat until tender. Cool; slice or shred chicken into bite-size pieces. Discard bones and skin. In a large bowl, combine remaining ingredients except broth and soup; toss to mix. Blend broth and one can soup; add to crumb mixture. Spray a slow cooker with non-stick vegetable spray. Spoon 1/2 can remaining soup into the bottom of slow cooker. Add alternate layers of chicken and dressing, ending with chicken. Top with remaining soup. Cover and cook on low setting for 3 hours. Serves 8 to 10.

A sit-down dinner every Sunday is a delightful way to bring the family together and share your blessings. Make it extra special with Mom's best lace tablecloth, Grandmother's sparkling silverware and fresh flowers in a vase...memories in the making!

White Chicken Chili

Mary Muchowicz
Elk Grove Village, IL

For my daughter's birthday party, we had such fun making crispy tortilla bowls and serving them with the chili.

1 to 2 16-oz. cans navy beans, drained and rinsed
4 14-1/2 oz. cans chicken broth
1 onion, chopped
2 cloves garlic, minced
1 T. ground cumin
1 T. dried oregano
1 t. salt
1 T. white pepper
1/4 t. ground cloves
1 c. water
5 c. cooked chicken, chopped
2 4-oz. cans chopped green chiles
Garnish: shredded Monterey Jack cheese, sour cream, salsa

Combine all ingredients except garnish in a large slow cooker. Cover and cook on low setting for 8 to 10 hours, or on high setting for 4 to 5 hours. To serve, ladle chili into tortilla bowls placed inside soup bowls. Top with cheese, sour cream and salsa. Makes 8 servings.

Tortilla Bowls:

For each bowl, use one 10-inch flour tortilla. Make 4 cuts in tortilla toward center, but not completely through. Set desired number of oven-proof soup bowls upside-down on a baking sheet. Press a tortilla over the outside of each bowl. Bake at 350 degrees for just a few minutes, until lightly golden. Let stand until cooled before removing from soup bowls.

Madge's Beefy Chili

Madge Shepard
Franklin, NC

A good bowl of chili is appreciated year 'round, but especially
in chilly weather! Serve with a cast-iron skillet of cornbread
or crisp corn chips...yum!

2 lbs. ground beef
1 green pepper, chopped
1 onion, chopped
16-oz. can kidney beans
15-1/2 oz. can diced tomatoes

10-oz. can chili-style diced
  tomatoes with green chiles
8-oz. can tomato sauce
1-oz. pkg. chili seasoning

In a large skillet, brown beef, pepper and onion together; drain. Mix beef mixture with remaining ingredients in a slow cooker. Cover and cook on low setting for 2 to 4 hours, until hot and well blended. Makes 6 to 8 servings.

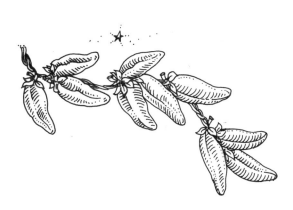

If you love super-spicy chili, give New Mexico chili powder a try.
Sold at Hispanic and specialty food stores, it contains pure
ground red chili peppers, unlike regular chili powder which is
a blend of chili, garlic and other seasonings.

Chicken & Bowties Dinner

Sena Horn
Payson, UT

Comfort food bubbling in the slow cooker...what could be better?
Garnish with a sprinkling of Parmesan cheese on top...scrumptious!

1/2 c. butter, sliced
4 to 5 boneless, skinless
  chicken breasts
2 .6-oz. pkgs. zesty Italian
  salad dressing mix
2 T. dried, minced onion
8-oz. pkg. cream cheese, cubed

2 10-3/4 oz. cans cream of
  chicken soup
12-oz. pkg. bowtie pasta,
  cooked
Optional: 10-oz. pkg. frozen
  baby peas, thawed

Place butter in the bottom of a slow cooker. Layer chicken breasts over butter; sprinkle with dressing mix and onion. Cover and cook on low setting for 4 to 5 hours. Remove chicken from slow cooker; dice into bite-size pieces and set aside. Add cream cheese and soup to slow cooker; stir together. Stir in chicken; cover and cook on high setting for 15 minutes, until sauce is warmed through. Add cooked pasta and peas, if desired, to slow cooker and toss to mix well. Cover and let stand for several minutes until warmed through. Serves 6 to 8.

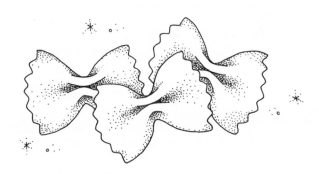

A red enamelware colander makes a delightful centerpiece
when filled with colorful ripe fruit...it's convenient
for healthy snacking too!

Sheryl's Beef Stroganoff

Sheryl Eastman
Highland, MI

I served this to my kids as they were growing up...my son would ask me for Beef Stroganoff all the time! It makes tasty leftovers for lunch the next day.

2 to 3 lbs. stew beef or round
  steak, cubed
1 to 2 T. olive oil
2 10-3/4 oz. cans cream of
  mushroom soup

2 T. all-purpose flour
4 cubes beef bouillon
8-oz. container sour cream
salt and pepper to taste
cooked rice or egg noodles

In a skillet over medium heat, brown beef in oil. Drain; place into a slow cooker. Pour soup over beef; sprinkle flour on top and mix well. Add bouillon cubes and stir well again. Cover and cook on low setting for 7 to 9 hours. Stir twice while cooking. When beef is tender, add sour cream and mix well. Cover and cook on low setting for about 30 minutes, until heated through. Add salt and pepper to taste. Serve over cooked rice or noodles. Serves 4 to 6.

A time-saving tip...slice & dice meats and veggies
the night before, place in separate plastic zipping bags and
pop in the fridge. In the morning, toss everything into
the slow cooker and you're on your way.

3-Cheese Baked Penne

Jennie Gist
Gooseberry Patch

Good enough for company...don't tell 'em how easy it was!

1 lb. ground beef	15-oz. container ricotta cheese
1 onion, chopped	1 c. grated Parmesan cheese
2 t. Italian seasoning	2 c. shredded mozzarella
1/2 t. salt	cheese, divided
2 26-oz. jars spaghetti sauce	16-oz. pkg. penne pasta, cooked

Brown beef and onion in a large skillet over medium heat; drain. Stir in seasonings; add sauce and set aside. Blend ricotta, Parmesan and one cup mozzarella cheese. Spread 2 cups of sauce mixture in the bottom of a slow cooker; top with 2 cups cooked pasta. Layer half of cheese mixture over pasta. Layer with 2 cups sauce, remaining pasta, remaining cheese mixture and remaining sauce. Cover and cook on low setting for 6 to 7 hours. Shortly before serving time, sprinkle with remaining mozzarella cheese. Cover and let stand until cheese is melted, about 10 minutes. Serves 6 to 8.

To cook up perfect pasta, fill a large pot with water and bring to a rolling boil. Add a tablespoon of salt, if desired. Stir in pasta; return to a rolling boil. Boil, uncovered, for the time recommended on package. There's no need to add oil... frequent stirring will keep pasta from sticking together.

Mark's Spaghetti & Meatballs

Patti Walker
Mocksville, NC

After returning home from a trip overseas, my husband couldn't wait to prepare supper for our family. He had watched a similar recipe being shown on the plane and was ready to try it on his family. He made the most delicious spaghetti & meatballs that I had ever eaten...try it and I'm sure you will agree!

1-1/2 lbs. lean ground beef
20-oz. pkg. Italian pork sausage
   links, removed from casings
3 slices dry bread, torn into
   crumbs
1 egg, beaten
1/3 c. onion, finely sliced

1/4 c. grated Parmesan cheese
1 t. Italian seasoning
45-oz. jar pasta sauce, divided
16-oz. pkg. spaghetti, cooked
Garnish: grated Parmesan
   cheese

Combine beef, sausage, bread crumbs, egg, onion, cheese, seasoning and 1/3 cup pasta sauce in a large bowl. Mix well; form into one-inch meatballs. Spoon a little sauce over the bottom of a slow cooker. Place meatballs on top of sauce. If more than one layer is made, add a little sauce between layers. Top with half of remaining sauce. Cover and cook on high setting for 2 hours; turn down to low setting and continue cooking for 2 to 6 hours. If desired, remove any grease on top with a paper towel or a slice of bread. Stir in remaining sauce about 30 minutes before serving time; keep slow cooker on low setting. To serve, divide cooked spaghetti among dinner plates. Top with sauce, 3 to 4 meatballs and a sprinkling of cheese. Serves 6 to 8.

Use a vegetable peeler to quickly cut thin curls from a block of Parmesan cheese for garnishing pasta or salads.

Tuscan Beef Stew

Jean DePerna
Fairport, NY

One morning I tossed a few things together and this delicious dish was the result...I have been asked to make it ever since!

2 lbs. stew beef, cubed
2 to 3 T. oil
10-3/4 oz. can tomato soup
10-1/2 oz. can beef broth
1/2 c. dry red wine or water
2 16-oz. cans cannellini beans, drained and rinsed

14-1/2 oz. can Italian-style diced tomatoes
3 carrots, cut into 1-inch pieces
1 t. Italian seasoning
1/2 t. garlic powder

In a large skillet over medium-high heat, brown beef in oil; drain. Transfer beef to a slow cooker; add remaining ingredients and stir to mix. Cover and cook on low setting for 8 to 9 hours. Serves 6.

Brightly colored vintage-style oilcloth makes the best-ever tablecloth...it wipes clean in a jiffy!

Savory Porketta Stew

Samantha Starks
Madison, WI

When I was growing up in a big Italian family in Minnesota, my grandmother's porketta roast was always a favorite, so I was happy to find this easy recipe that captures the flavor of her roast. Sometimes I omit the vegetables and just prepare the seasoned roast, then shred the pork and spoon it onto hard rolls, topped with grainy mustard. Deliciozo!

1 lb. new redskin potatoes	2 T. olive oil
2 green peppers, cubed	1 c. beef broth
1 c. baby carrots	6-oz. pkg. au jus gravy mix
1/2 c. onion, chopped	1 T. fennel seed
2 T. garlic, minced	1 T. Italian seasoning
2-1/2 lb. boneless pork shoulder	3 T. all-purpose flour
roast, cubed	1/4 c. cold water

Place vegetables and garlic in a slow cooker. In a large skillet over medium-high heat, brown pork in oil; drain. Add pork to slow cooker and set aside. Add broth, gravy mix, fennel seed and Italian seasoning to skillet. Cook and stir briefly, scraping up any browned bits from bottom. Pour over pork in slow cooker. Cover and cook on low setting for 8 to 10 hours. About 20 minutes before serving time, whisk flour and water together in a small bowl. Whisk mixture into stew. Turn slow cooker to high setting. Cook, stirring occasionally, until thickened, about 15 minutes. Makes 6 servings.

A family recipe book is a wonderful way to preserve one generation's traditions for the next. At the next family reunion, ask everyone to bring copies of their most-requested recipes, just the way they make them. Combine all the recipes into a book and have enough copies made for everyone!

Shipwreck Stew

Sharon Tillman
Hampton, VA

My boys were always such picky eaters...unless there was Shipwreck Stew for dinner! The recipe's unusual name really fascinated them, and they would eat every bite.

1 lb. ground beef, browned
  and drained
2 16-oz. cans kidney beans
10-3/4 oz. can tomato soup
5 potatoes, peeled and cubed
1/2 green pepper, diced

1/2 onion, diced
1/4 c. long-cooking rice,
  uncooked
1 t. Worcestershire sauce
1 t. chili powder
1 c. water

Combine all ingredients in a slow cooker; mix well. Cover and cook on high setting for 4 to 6 hours. Serves 6.

Decorate a pillar candle with sparkly sand and tiny seashells brought back from a trip to the beach. Simply brush craft glue on the candle, sprinkle with sand and press in shells. Set the candle on a saucer filled with more sand...so pretty!

Country Chicken Chowder

Kimberly Hancock
Murrieta, CA

This chowder is a snap to make and oh-so hearty...it's a meal in a bowl! Garnish individual servings with a dollop of sour cream and a sprinkle of dill weed.

2 T. butter
1-1/2 lbs. chicken tenders,
  sliced into 1/2-inch pieces
2 10-3/4 oz. cans cream of
  potato soup
1-1/2 c. chicken broth

2 onions, chopped
2 stalks celery, sliced
2 carrots, peeled and sliced
2 c. frozen corn
1 t. dill weed
1/2 c. half-and-half

Melt butter in a skillet over medium heat. Add chicken and cook until golden. Place chicken in a slow cooker; stir in remaining ingredients except half-and-half. Cover and cook on low setting for 3 to 4 hours. Shortly before serving time, turn off slow cooker; stir in half-and-half. Cover and let stand for 5 to 10 minutes, just until heated through. Serves 8.

Are you preparing a recipe that calls for thin strips of chicken or beef? Pop it in the freezer for 10 to 15 minutes, until slightly frozen...it will slice in a jiffy.

Savory Slow Cookers

Sweet-and-Sour Pork

Janice Dorsey
San Antonio, TX

We really like this toss & go recipe...it's equally good with cubes of boneless chicken breast.

1-1/2 lbs. boneless pork loin, cubed
1 green pepper, chopped
1 onion, chopped
14-oz. can pineapple chunks, drained

14-1/2 oz. can chicken broth
10-oz. bottle sweet-and-sour sauce
cooked rice

Place pork cubes in a slow cooker; top with remaining ingredients except rice. Cover and cook on low setting for 6 to 7 hours, or on high setting for 4 hours. Serve over cooked rice. Makes 6 servings.

Let the kids lend a hand in the kitchen! Preschoolers can wash veggies, fold napkins and set the table. Older children can measure, shred, chop, stir and maybe even help with meal planning and grocery shopping.

Pepper Steak

Stephanie Westfall
Dallas, GA

*A family favorite! Sprinkle with chow mein noodles
if you like a crunchy topping.*

1-1/2 to 2 lbs. beef round steak, sliced into strips
15-oz. can diced tomatoes
1 to 2 red peppers, sliced
1 onion, chopped

4-oz. can sliced mushrooms, drained
1/4 c. salsa
cooked rice

Mix all ingredients except rice in a slow cooker. Cover and cook on low setting for 6 to 8 hours. To serve, spoon over cooked rice. Makes 4 to 6 servings.

Dress up dinner with frilly green onion curls. Cut the green tops into long, thin slices. Soak in ice water for 15 minutes and they'll curl open.

Homestyle Chicken Stew

Jennifer Oglesby
Brownsville, IN

This is so good on a chilly autumn or winter day, along with homemade bread...mmm! If you don't have any celery on hand, just add 1/2 teaspoon celery seed from the spice rack.

1 lb. boneless, skinless chicken breasts, cubed
2 c. potatoes, peeled and cubed
1 stalk celery, sliced
2 carrots, peeled and sliced
14-1/2 oz. can chicken broth

6-oz. can tomato paste
1/2 t. paprika
1/4 t. pepper
1/4 t. dried thyme
1-1/2 T. cold water
1 T. cornstarch

In a slow cooker, combine all ingredients except water and cornstarch. Mix together well. Cover and cook on low setting for 7 to 8 hours, or on high setting for 3-1/2 hours. About 30 minutes before serving time, stir water and cornstarch together and stir into stew. Cook, covered, for an additional 30 minutes, or until thickened. Serves 4.

It's easy to keep rolls nice and warm during dinner. Before arranging rolls in a bread basket, place a terra cotta warming tile in the bottom and line with a homespun tea towel. Now pass the butter, please!

Mushroom-Barley Chicken

Diana Chaney
Olathe, KS

There's something that's just so comforting about barley!

2 lbs. chicken
2 T. butter
2 c. sliced mushrooms
1 c. pearled barley, uncooked
2 carrots, peeled and chopped
1 onion, chopped

1 stalk celery, chopped
14-1/2 oz. can chicken broth
1 t. poultry seasoning
1 bay leaf
1/4 t. salt
1/4 t. pepper

In a large skillet, brown chicken pieces in butter over medium-high heat, turning occasionally. Drain. Combine remaining ingredients in a slow cooker. Add chicken; stir. Cover and cook on low setting for 6 to 8 hours. Discard bay leaf before serving. Makes 6 servings.

Whimsical vintage salt & pepper shakers add a dash of fun at mealtime. Look for them at flea markets or thrift shops... you're sure to find some favorites.

Angela's Tortilla Stack

Angela Cradic
Kingsport, TN

We like to think of this yummy dish as Mexican lasagna.

1 lb. ground beef, browned
   and drained
5 to 6 6-inch corn tortillas,
   each cut into 6 wedges
10-3/4 oz. can Cheddar
   cheese soup

1-1/4 oz. pkg. taco seasoning
   mix
2 tomatoes, chopped
Garnish: sour cream, shredded
   lettuce

Crumble 1/4 of browned beef into the bottom of a slow cooker. Top
with 1/4 of tortilla wedges. In a small bowl, blend soup and seasoning
mix, using 2/3 to all of seasoning mix as desired. Spread 1/4 of soup
mixture over tortillas. Sprinkle with 1/4 of tomatoes. Repeat layering
until all ingredients are used. Cover and cook on low setting for 4 to
5 hours. Spoon onto individual plates. Top each serving with sour
cream and lettuce as desired. Makes 4 servings.

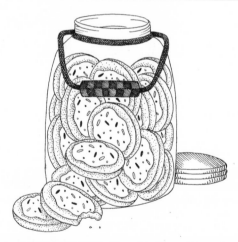

While supper is simmering in the slow cooker, there's time to do
other things. Why not bake up a double batch of cookies? There will
be plenty for dessert and extras to share with a neighbor, babysitter
or anyone else who would love to know you're thinking of them!

Cozy Casseroles

Heavenly Chicken

Lynn Wright
Pleasant Prairie, WI

This casserole is so delicious...a good meal for Sunday afternoon!
It makes the whole house smell wonderful while it's in the oven.
Just add some steamed broccoli and dinner is ready.

6 boneless, skinless chicken
   breasts
8-oz. pkg. sliced Swiss cheese
2 10-3/4 oz. cans cream of
   chicken soup

1-3/4 c. stuffing mix
1 c. butter, melted

Place chicken breasts in a lightly greased 13"x9" baking pan.
Arrange cheese slices over chicken, covering to edges. Spread soup
over cheese, extending to edges. Sprinkle with stuffing mix; drizzle
melted butter over stuffing. Cover and bake at 300 degrees for one
hour. Uncover; continue baking for one additional hour. Serves 6.

A handy chart in case you don't have the exact size
pan or dish called for...

13"x9" baking pan = 3-quart casserole dish
9"x9" baking pan = 2-quart casserole dish
8"x8" baking pan = 1-1/2 quart casserole dish

Darlene's Chicken & Rice

Darlene Kaminski
Huntley, IL

This is a delicious winter meal that is so easy to make and clean up. It's one of the first meals I made for my husband. We've been married for 36 years now and it is still one of his favorites.

10-3/4 oz. can cream of
   mushroom soup
10-3/4 oz. can cream of
   chicken soup
10-3/4 oz. can cream of celery
   soup

1-1/2 c. long-cooking rice,
   uncooked
6 chicken thighs

In a large bowl, mix soups together. Add uncooked rice and mix well. Spread rice mixture in an aluminum foil-lined, lightly greased roasting pan. Place chicken thighs on top of rice mixture; cover pan with aluminum foil. Bake at 350 degrees for one hour. Carefully remove foil and stir rice mixture. Return to oven for 15 minutes, covering pan again if rice isn't tender. Serves 3 to 4.

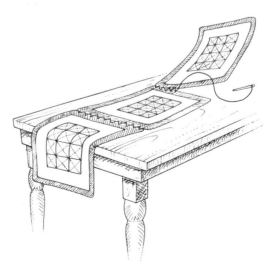

Whip up a country-style table runner in a jiffy! Just stitch several quilted placemats end-to-end.

Easy Cottage Pie

Kay Snyder
Cuba, NY

My girls just love this version of a shepherd's pie!
It's different and quick to fix.

1-1/2 to 2 lbs. ground beef
16-oz. can Sloppy Joe sauce
14-oz. pkg. instant mashed
  potato flakes

1-1/2 c. shredded Cheddar or
  American cheese

In a skillet over medium heat, brown beef. Drain; add sauce to beef and heat through. Spread mixture in the bottom of an ungreased 13"x9" baking pan. Prepare 12 servings of mashed potatoes as package directs. Carefully spread potatoes over beef mixture; top with cheese. Bake, uncovered, at 350 degrees until cheese melts. Serves 8 to 10.

Keep a picnic basket packed with a blanket, tableware and other picnic supplies. You'll be ready to pack up an easy-to-tote casserole dinner, load everyone into the car and take off for a picnic at a moment's notice!

Angie's Taco Pie

*Angie Krebs
Ashland, OH*

*This was just a quick toss-together recipe. I tried a little of this
and a little of that...it was a hit with my family!*

8-1/2 oz. pkg. cornbread muffin
  mix
1/2 lb. ground beef
1-1/4 oz. pkg. taco seasoning
  mix

8-oz. jar salsa
3/4 c. shredded Cheddar cheese

Prepare cornbread mix according to package directions. Pour batter
into a greased 10" pie plate and set aside. Brown beef in a skillet;
drain and stir in taco seasoning. Spoon beef mixture over batter;
top with salsa and cheese. Bake, uncovered, at 400 degrees for
20 to 25 minutes, until cheese melts and cornbread sets. Serves 8.

On a dry-erase message board, use a permanent-ink pen
to list kitchen staples like milk, bread, cheese and eggs.
Post the board on the fridge. Check off items with a dry-erase
pen as they are almost used up...how clever!

Hearty Pierogie Casserole

Sheryl Maksymowski
Grand Rapids, MI

I have been making this casserole for nearly 25 years and my family's faces still light up every time I make it. It's comfort food that sticks to your ribs and it is so very easy!

2 to 3 16.9-oz. pkgs. frozen
    favorite-flavor pierogies
1-1/2 to 2 lbs. smoked pork
    sausage, sliced into bite-size
    pieces

26-oz. can cream of mushroom
    soup
3-1/4 c. milk
2 to 3 c. shredded Cheddar
    cheese

Bring a large saucepan of water to a boil; add pierogies and sausage. Cook for 5 to 7 minutes, until pierogies float; drain. Arrange mixture in a 13"x9" glass baking pan that has been sprayed with non-stick vegetable spray. Blend soup and milk; pour over top. Top with cheese. Bake, uncovered, at 350 degrees for 30 to 35 minutes, or until soup is bubbly and cheese is lightly golden. Let stand for about 5 minutes before serving. Makes 8 servings.

If you're taking a casserole along to a potluck or carry-in, secure the lid with a brightly colored tea towel wrapped around the baking dish and knotted at the top. Keep the serving spoon handy by tucking it through the knot.

Man-O-Manicotti

Rebecca Humes
Saint Louis, MO

My mother would always fix this recipe on wintry Saturdays and put it in the refrigerator. After church on Sunday she popped it in the oven...soon supper would be waiting!

1 lb. ground beef, browned and
   drained
8-oz. pkg. manicotti shells,
   uncooked

26-oz. jar spaghetti sauce
2 c. shredded mozzarella cheese

Spoon browned beef into uncooked manicotti shells. Arrange 2 rows of manicotti in a 13"x9" baking pan that has been sprayed with non-stick vegetable spray. Pour sauce over manicotti; sprinkle with cheese. Cover and bake at 350 degrees for one hour. Serves 4.

When packing a tomato-based casserole to share with a friend or neighbor, tuck in a small can of tomato juice too. Add a note to drizzle the juice over the casserole just before reheating. The casserole will be extra moist and flavorful when it's reheated.

John's Spinach & Red Pepper Chicken
Michelle Johnson
Drexel Hill, PA

My brother-in-law's cousin John shared this recipe with me...it's a keeper! I like to prepare this casserole in the morning, pop it in the fridge and bake it when I come home from work.

6 boneless, skinless chicken
  breasts
12-oz. jar roasted red peppers,
  drained
10-oz. pkg. frozen chopped
  spinach, thawed and drained

8-oz. pkg. shredded Italian
  cheese blend
8-oz. bottle Italian salad
  dressing
cooked rice or pasta

Place chicken breasts between 2 pieces of wax paper and pound to flatten. Lay chicken in a lightly greased 13"x9" baking pan. Arrange peppers on top of chicken; layer with spinach and cheese. Pour dressing over top. Cover and refrigerate for one to 8 hours. Bake, uncovered, at 350 degrees for 30 minutes. Serve over cooked rice or pasta. Makes 6 servings.

Take an after-dinner walk. In springtime, look for the first spring flowers popping from the ground...in fall, see who can spot the first tree to turn! Any time of year, take a look all around you as you stroll...it's a super way to get to know your neighborhood better.

Italian Stuffed Peppers

Vivian Gray
North Charleroi, PA

*My grandmother made these when I was a child. She lived upstairs and
I would always run up to see what she was cooking. If these peppers
were being made, I knew where I'd be eating supper!*

4 red, yellow or green peppers,
   tops removed
14-1/2 oz. can stewed tomatoes
4 slices white bread, cubed

8-oz. pkg. Longhorn or mild
   Cheddar cheese, cubed
salt and pepper to taste

Cut off a thin slice from bottoms of peppers if necessary so they will
stand up. Place peppers in a microwave-safe container; pour 2 inches
water around peppers. Cover with plastic wrap; microwave on high
setting for 3 minutes, just until softened. Drain and set aside. Mix
remaining ingredients and stir, adding a little water if needed to ensure
bread is well moistened. Stuff peppers with mixture. Arrange in a
one-quart casserole dish that has been sprayed with non-stick
vegetable spray. Add 1/2 inch water to dish, pouring around peppers.
Bake, covered, at 350 degrees for 30 to 35 minutes, until peppers
are tender and heated through. Serves 4.

Stuffed green peppers will stand upright nicely
when arranged in a Bundt® pan before baking.

Zesty Parmesan Chicken

Lisa Ludwig
Fort Wayne, IN

The juiciest, most flavorful chicken I've ever tasted!

1/2 c. grated Parmesan cheese
1/2 t. garlic powder
.75 env. Italian salad dressing
   mix

4 to 6 boneless, skinless
   chicken breasts

Mix all dry ingredients together. Coat chicken in mixture; place in a greased shallow 13"x9" baking pan. Bake, uncovered, at 400 degrees for 25 to 30 minutes, until juices run clear. Serves 4 to 6.

Rosemary New Potatoes

Tina Dillon
Parma, OH

The best way to savor tiny new potatoes...roasted in olive oil, with a hint of garlic and rosemary.

1-1/2 lbs. new redskin potatoes
1/4 c. olive oil
4 to 6 cloves garlic, pressed

1 T. fresh rosemary, snipped
salt and pepper to taste

Peel off a strip around each potato, if desired. Mix remaining ingredients in a large bowl. Add potatoes and toss well to coat. Place potatoes in an ungreased shallow 13"x9" baking pan. Bake, uncovered, at 450 degrees for 30 to 40 minutes, until potatoes are tender. Makes 4 to 6 servings.

Delci's Crispy Chicken

Delci Whalen
Post Falls, ID

*This is a favorite recipe in my family. It was given to me as
a bridal shower gift in a scrapbooked cookbook. To crush
the cereal easily, place it in a bag and roll with a rolling pin.*

6 chicken thighs
1/4 to 1/2 c. butter, melted

5 c. crispy rice cereal, crushed
salt and pepper to taste

Line a broiler pan with aluminum foil; coat with non-stick vegetable
spray and set aside. Dip chicken in melted butter, then into crushed
cereal to coat. Place on broiler pan; add salt and pepper to taste. Set
pan on middle rack of oven. Bake, uncovered, at 350 degrees for
about 50 minutes, until chicken juices run clear when pierced.
Makes 6 servings.

Cottage Potato Puff

Ruie Richardson
Marinette, WI

Turn ordinary mashed potato flakes into something special.

14-oz. pkg. instant mashed
  potato flakes
1 T. dried, minced onion

8-oz. container cottage cheese
1 T. butter, diced
Garnish: paprika

Prepare 4 servings of potatoes according to package directions, adding
onion to the boiling water called for. Fold in cottage cheese. Turn into
a lightly buttered one-quart casserole dish. Dot with butter; sprinkle
with a little paprika. Bake, uncovered, at 350 degrees for 30 minutes,
or until top is lightly golden. Serves 5.

Before crumb-coating or dredging meat, lay a piece of
wax paper on the counter. When you're done, just fold up
the paper and toss away the mess!

Grandma Hodges' Chile Rice

Mary Ann Hodges
Alexandria, VA

Comfort food that brings back fond memories...delicious with grilled chicken or hamburgers.

1 c. sour cream
4-oz. can chopped green chiles
8-oz. pkg. shredded Monterey
  Jack cheese
8-oz. pkg. shredded Cheddar
  cheese

1 c. long-cooking rice, cooked
  and divided
salt and pepper to taste

Mix sour cream and chiles. In a separate bowl, toss cheeses together. Place half of cooked rice in the bottom of a buttered 9"x9" baking pan. Spread half of sour cream mixture over rice. Top with half of cheese mixture. Repeat with remaining ingredients for a second layer. Cover loosely with aluminum foil. Bake at 325 degrees for 30 minutes. Uncover and bake 15 minutes more. Serves 4.

Start a kitchen journal that's part cookbook, part keepsake.
Decorate a blank book, then write or paste in recipes
you've tried. Add notes about family members' favorites and
who was visiting for dinner...even add snapshots.
You'll love looking back on these happy memories!

Mushroom-Rice Pilaf

Cathy Toogood
Clinton, PA

My mother made this rice dish for as long as I can remember. We all loved its buttery onion and mushroom flavor. Now it's a favorite of mine for family meals, covered dish dinners and picnics too.

1/2 c. butter, sliced
1-1/2 c. long-cooking rice, uncooked
10-1/2 oz. can French onion soup

1-1/4 c. water
1 cube beef bouillon, crumbled
7-oz. can sliced mushrooms, drained

Add butter to an 11"x9" baking pan; place in a 350-degree oven until melted. Stir in uncooked rice until evenly coated. Add remaining ingredients and stir slowly until well mixed. Bake, covered, at 350 degrees for 40 minutes. Stir occasionally. Makes 6 servings.

If you want to try a casserole recipe but it's too large for your small family, here's an idea. Just divide the casserole ingredients into two smaller dishes and freeze one to enjoy later.

Caesar's Pork Chops & Potatoes

Nancy Rawle
Springfield, MA

This delicious recipe came from my Italian grandfather. It's perfect for weekends...just slide it in the oven, enjoy the afternoon and then gather everyone for a savory meal they'll love.

6 to 8 bone-in pork chops
5 c. potatoes, peeled and cubed
garlic powder, salt and pepper
   to taste

1/4 c. all-purpose flour

In a greased large roasting pan, arrange pork chops in a single layer. Spread potatoes over pork chops. Sprinkle seasonings and flour over top. Add enough water to cover. Bake, uncovered, at 350 degrees for about 4 to 5 hours, until sauce thickens and potatoes are crispy. Makes 6 to 8 servings.

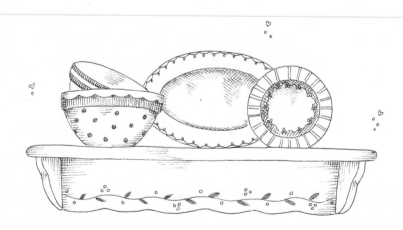

Versatile serving pieces that can be used year 'round in different ways mean more fun at the table, with fewer items to store. An apple-red serving platter can star at a 4th of July picnic, a birthday dinner and again at Christmastime.

Yummy Pork Chops

Renae Scheiderer
Beallsville, OH

This recipe was given to me when I first married...
it's still a family favorite!

4 pork loin chops, 1/2-inch
   thick
3 T. soy sauce

3 T. catsup
2 t. honey

Place pork chops in an ungreased 8"x8" baking pan. Mix remaining ingredients together; pour over pork chops. Cover and bake at 350 degrees for about 45 minutes, or until pork is just slightly pink in center. Uncover; bake an additional 5 minutes. Makes 4 servings.

Country Corn Casserole

Tammie Burdeshaw
Abbeville, AL

A favorite for potlucks and holiday meals.

15-1/4 oz. can corn, drained
14-3/4 oz. can creamed corn
1/4 c. butter, melted

2 T. all-purpose flour
2 T. sugar

Mix all ingredients together. Transfer to a greased 13"x9" baking pan. Bake, uncovered, at 350 degrees for 30 minutes, until hot and bubbly. Serves 6 to 8.

Dust off Mom's vintage casserole dishes...they're just right for baking family-pleasing hearty casseroles, with a side dish of sweet memories.

Hot Dog Haystacks

Jamie Pruitt
Peru, IL

*My husband shared this yummy, quick recipe with me before
we were married. It was one of his old family favorites...
now we make it all the time!*

6 hot dogs
6 hot dog buns, split

6 c. mashed potatoes, warmed
1 c. shredded Colby Jack cheese

Cook hot dogs in boiling water. Drain; split in half lengthwise. Arrange split buns on an ungreased baking sheet. Top each bun half with a hot dog half. Cover generously with warm mashed potatoes. Sprinkle with shredded cheese. Bake, uncovered, at 350 degrees for 30 minutes. Serves 6.

Make a trivet to protect the tabletop from hot dishes in a jiffy.
Simply attach a cork or felt square to the bottom of
a large ceramic tile with craft glue.

Cheesy Hot Dog Bake

Tina Bumgardner
Toledo, OH

When my son was little, we came up with this recipe together. We both enjoy it and it's so easy to put together.

8 hot dogs, sliced
2 11-oz. cans corn, drained
10-3/4 oz. can Cheddar cheese
   soup

6.6-oz. pkg. instant mashed
   potato flakes, prepared
1 c. shredded Cheddar cheese

Place hot dogs in a lightly greased 9"x9" baking pan. Add corn and soup; mix well. Spread mashed potatoes over top and sprinkle with cheese. Bake, uncovered, at 350 degrees for 20 to 30 minutes, until cheese has melted and edges start to bubble. Serves 4.

Watch for whimsical diner-style sectioned plates at tag sales and antique shops. They're perfect for serving up kid-size portions of casseroles...the sections keep the casserole and side dishes separate.

Easy Ham & Potato Casserole

Kay Bradshaw
Rose Hill, NC

A scrumptious way to serve leftover holiday ham. To make it a complete meal, add a drained can of green beans.

2 c. cooked ham, diced
30-oz. pkg. frozen diced
   potatoes, thawed
10-3/4 oz. can cream of
   mushroom soup

10-3/4 oz. can Cheddar cheese
   soup
salt and pepper to taste

Mix all ingredients together. Transfer to a lightly greased 9"x9" baking pan. Bake, uncovered, at 375 degrees for 45 to 60 minutes, until heated through. Makes 6 servings.

To enjoy the flavor of Life, take big bites.

- Robert Heilein

A busy-day hint...if family members will be eating at different times, spoon casserole ingredients into individual ramekins for baking. Each person can enjoy their own fresh-from-the-oven mini casserole.

Stephanie's Kielbasa Dinner

Stephanie Donaghe
Searcy, AR

*I came up with this recipe when I was single and money was tight...
it tastes just as good the next day as leftovers. For variety,
sliced onion and squash are delicious additions.*

1 lb. Kielbasa, sliced
3 to 4 redskin potatoes, cubed

1-1/2 c. baby carrots
seasoned salt to taste

Spray a 2-quart casserole dish with non-stick vegetable spray. Add
Kielbasa, potatoes and carrots. Sprinkle with salt and toss to coat;
sprinkle a little more salt on top. Cover dish with aluminum foil
and cut several vents. Bake at 350 degrees for about 60 minutes,
checking for doneness after 45 minutes. Some carrots may take up
to 75 minutes to become fork-tender. Serves 6.

Sauerkraut & Noodle Bake

Jen Stout
Blandon, PA

Oh-so simple and satisfying.

1 lb. ground pork sausage
15-oz. can diced tomatoes
32-oz. pkg. sauerkraut, drained

16-oz. pkg. medium egg
noodles, cooked

Brown sausage in a skillet over medium heat. Drain; add tomatoes
with juice and sauerkraut. Cook together for 15 minutes. Combine
sausage mixture and cooked noodles; place in a lightly greased
13"x9" baking pan. Bake, uncovered, at 350 degrees for 40 minutes.
Serves 6.

Cook noodles that will be used in casseroles for the shorter time
indicated on the package. They will become tender
while the casserole bakes.

Heavenly Haddock

Christy Jones
Barrington, NH

This yummy dish was made for my dad when he was a child, my mother made it for me and now I make it for my own family! Everyone who tries it, loves it.

2 lbs. haddock fillets, thawed
   if frozen
16-oz. container sour cream

garlic salt to taste
2 T. lemon juice
6-oz. can French fried onions

Rinse fish fillets and pat dry. Arrange in a lightly greased 13"x9" baking pan. Combine sour cream, garlic salt and lemon juice; spread mixture over fish. Top with onions. Cover with aluminum foil and bake at 350 degrees for 25 minutes. Remove foil and allow to bake for an additional 10 minutes, until onions are crisp. Serves 6.

Out of dried bread crumbs for breading chicken or fish? Try instant mashed potato flakes for a tasty, quick substitute.

Greek Tilapia with Orzo

Claire Bertram
Lexington, KY

One of my mom's friends gave her this tasty recipe. All kinds of fish like flounder, sole or perch work well in it.

1-1/2 lbs. tilapia fillets, thawed
   if frozen
juice and zest of 1 lemon
1 T. fresh oregano, snipped

salt and pepper to taste
1 pt. cherry tomatoes, halved
8-oz. pkg. orzo pasta, cooked

Rinse fish fillets and pat dry. Place in a lightly greased 13"x9" baking pan. Sprinkle fish evenly with lemon juice and zest, oregano, salt and pepper. Arrange tomatoes around fish; cover with aluminum foil. Bake at 400 degrees for 16 to 18 minutes, until fish is opaque and tomatoes are tender. Serve over cooked orzo, drizzled with juices from baking pan. Serves 4.

Crisp coleslaw pairs well with fish dishes. Blend a bag of shredded coleslaw mix with 1/2 cup mayonnaise, 2 tablespoons milk, one tablespoon vinegar and 1/2 teaspoon sugar. For a yummy variation, toss in some mandarin oranges. Chill for about one hour before serving.

Little Red Hen

Pennie Eisenbeis
Kasson, MN

My family just loves this dish on a cold Minnesota evening...it warms us right up! The sweet red dressing blends so nicely with the potatoes and chicken. It's an easy make-ahead dish...you can fix it the night before, then pop it in a hot oven after work.

3 to 4 lbs. skinless chicken
4 to 6 potatoes, peeled and cut
   into bite-size pieces
1 onion, diced

16-oz. bottle western-style
   salad dressing
salt and pepper to taste

Place chicken pieces, potatoes and onion in a 13"x9" baking pan that has been sprayed with non-stick vegetable spray. Drizzle salad dressing over all ingredients. Cover with aluminum foil. Bake at 350 degrees for 30 minutes. Remove foil and bake for an additional 30 minutes, until chicken juices run clear and potatoes are tender. Serves 4 to 6.

Add the words "You Are Special Today" around the rim of a dinner plate with a glass paint pen. Reserve it for family birthdays and graduations...even for small accomplishments like a child learning to tie her shoes. It's sure to become a cherished tradition.

Special Apricot Chicken

Kathleen Rampy
Midlothian, TX

Super-easy comfort food! I make this often to take to a family with a new baby, a friend who's recovering from surgery or just because! It's excellent with brown rice and green beans.

8 boneless, skinless chicken
  breasts
6-oz. jar apricot preserves

1/2 c. Italian salad dressing
1.35-oz. pkg. onion soup mix

Arrange chicken breasts in a lightly greased 13"x9" baking pan. Mix remaining ingredients and spoon over chicken. Bake, uncovered, at 350 degrees for about one hour, until chicken juices run clear. Makes 8 servings.

Set a photo placecard at each person's place setting. Use alphabet pasta to spell out names on mini picture frames and tuck in photos...clever!

Crazy Macaroni Bake

Cheran Salvaggio
Lithia Springs, GA

A fun recipe using mixed-up pasta in fun shapes.

1 lb. ground beef, browned and
drained
12-oz. pkg. 4-shape tricolor
pasta, cooked

26-oz. jar garlic and herb
spaghetti sauce
2 c. shredded sharp Cheddar
cheese

Stir together browned beef, cooked pasta and sauce. Transfer to a
13"x9" baking pan that has been coated with non-stick vegetable
spray. Sprinkle cheese over top. Bake, uncovered, at 350 degrees for
30 minutes, until heated through and cheese is melted. Serves 6.

Meatless Baked Spaghetti

Rose Defibaugh
Kearneysville, WV

*My mother-in-law gave me this recipe 30 years ago. It became a
favorite for my children and now for my granddaughter too.*

16-oz. pkg. spaghetti, cooked
1 c. grated Parmesan cheese
16-oz. pkg. shredded
mozzarella cheese, divided

Garnish: favorite spaghetti
sauce, warmed

Toss cooked spaghetti with Parmesan cheese. Layer half of spaghetti
mixture in a well greased 13"x9" pan; cover with half of mozzarella
cheese. Add remaining spaghetti mixture; top with remaining cheese.
Bake, uncovered, at 350 degrees for 20 minutes, until heated
through. Cut into squares; serve topped with warm spaghetti sauce.
Makes 6 to 8 servings.

3-Cheese Ravioli

Mary Gage
Wakewood, CA

This recipe was a great discovery...it's really easy to prepare, but bakes up like lasagna. Make it your own by using your favorite flavors of spaghetti sauce and ravioli.

28-oz. jar spaghetti sauce, divided
25-oz. pkg. frozen cheese ravioli, cooked
16-oz. container cottage cheese, divided

16-oz. pkg. shredded mozzarella cheese, divided
1/4 c. grated Parmesan cheese

Spread 1/2 cup sauce in the bottom of an ungreased 11"x7" baking pan. Layer with half of the ravioli, 1-1/4 cups sauce, one cup cottage cheese and 2 cups mozzarella cheese. Repeat layers. Sprinkle with Parmesan cheese. Bake, uncovered, at 350 degrees for 30 to 40 minutes, or until hot and bubbly. Let stand for 5 to 10 minutes before serving. Makes 8 servings.

A fresh salad is right at home alongside cheesy baked pasta casseroles. Toss together mixed greens, cherry tomatoes and thinly sliced red onion in a salad bowl. Whisk together 1/4 cup each of balsamic vinegar and olive oil, then drizzle over salad...so zesty!

Cheesy Chicken Chalupas

Carrie Kiiskila
Racine, WI

*Everybody loves this hearty Mexican dish! Toss hot cooked rice
with salsa and cheese for a quick & easy side.*

2 10-3/4 oz. cans cream of
   chicken soup
16-oz. container sour cream
4-oz. can diced green chiles
2-1/4 oz. can chopped black
   olives, drained
3 green onions, chopped

1 onion, chopped
3 c. shredded Cheddar cheese
4 to 5 chicken breasts, cooked
   and diced
10 to 12 10-inch flour tortillas
2 c. shredded Monterey Jack
   cheese

Mix together soup, sour cream, vegetables and cheese in a large
bowl. Set aside 1-1/2 cups of soup mixture for topping; add chicken
to remaining mixture. Spoon chicken mixture into tortillas; roll up
and place into a 13"x9" baking pan coated with non-stick vegetable
spray. Spoon reserved soup mixture over tortillas; sprinkle with
Monterey Jack cheese. Bake, covered, at 350 degrees for one hour.
Makes 10 to 12 servings.

Feeding a crowd? Consider serving festive Mexican, Italian
or Chinese-style dishes that everybody loves. They usually feature
rice or pasta, so they're filling yet budget-friendly.
The theme makes it a snap to put together the menu
and table decorations too.

Hungry Man's Spanish Rice

Jeanette Payton
San Antonio, TX

I started making this recipe a zillion years ago, or so it seems!
At family get-togethers, there's never a spoonful left. My hubby
likes to eat it with flour tortillas.

1 lb. ground beef
Optional: 1/2 c. onion,
　chopped
Optional: 1/2 c. green pepper,
　chopped
garlic salt and seasoned salt
　to taste

6.8-oz. pkg. Spanish rice
　vermicelli mix, cooked
2 15-oz. cans ranch-style beans
8-oz. can tomato sauce
6 slices pasteurized process
　cheese, or 1-1/2 c. shredded
　Cheddar cheese

Brown beef in a skillet over medium heat, adding onion and green
pepper, if desired. Season beef to taste while cooking. Drain. Combine
beef mixture with remaining ingredients except cheese in a lightly
greased 3-quart casserole dish. Top with cheese. Bake, uncovered,
at 375 degrees for 30 to 45 minutes. Makes 6 servings.

First aid for casserole dishes with baked-on food spatters!
Mix equal amounts of cream of tartar and white vinegar into
a paste. Spread onto the dish and let stand for 30 minutes
to an hour. Spatters will wash off easily.

Baked Chicken Chimies

Jennifer Orme
Bluffdale, UT

*My husband absolutely loves this recipe! It's a scrumptious way
to use a rotisserie chicken. I like to freeze the chimichangas
and send them to work with him for lunch.*

1-1/2 c. cooked chicken, diced
1-1/3 c. shredded Cheddar
   cheese
1 c. southwest bean and corn
   picante salsa
1 t. ground cumin

1/2 t. dried oregano
6 10-inch flour tortillas
2 T. butter, melted
Garnish: shredded Cheddar
   cheese, chopped green onion,
   sour cream, salsa

Mix chicken, cheese, salsa and seasonings together. Spoon about
1/2 cup of mixture in the center of each tortilla. Fold opposite sides
over, then roll from the bottom up. Place tortillas seam-side down
on a lightly greased baking sheet. Brush with melted butter. Bake,
uncovered, for 25 minutes, until golden. Garnish with additional
cheese and onion. Serve with sour cream and salsa on the side.
Makes 6 servings.

Often, casserole recipes call for precooked chicken, ham or roast
beef. For a handy recipe shortcut, stop at the deli counter and
order thick-sliced meat...it's ready to cube or chop as needed.

Easy Oven Fajitas

Dianne Young
South Jordan, UT

*Great for gatherings! It's easy to prep everything ahead of time,
then pop it in the oven and enjoy your guests while it bakes.*

1-1/2 lbs. sliced stir-fry chicken
  and/or beef
1 green pepper, sliced
1 yellow pepper, sliced
1 onion, sliced
14-1/2 oz. can Mexican-
  seasoned stewed tomatoes

1 t. chili powder
1 t. ground cumin
8 to 12 6-inch flour tortillas,
  warmed
Garnish: sour cream, salsa

Spray a 15"x10" jelly-roll pan with non-stick vegetable spray.
Arrange meat and vegetables on pan in a single layer. Stir together
tomatoes with juice and seasonings; pour on top. Bake, uncovered,
at 375 degrees for 40 minutes, or until meat is cooked to desired
doneness. To serve, spoon onto warmed tortillas. Garnish as desired
and fold up. Serves 4 to 6.

Bless Our Home

Start family meals with a gratitude circle, in which each person
takes a moment to share 2 or 3 things that he or she
is thankful for that day. A sure way to put everyone in
a cheerful mood for dinner!

Johnny Marzetti

Brenda Montgomery
Lebanon, IN

A midwestern tradition! My mom used to make this when I was a kid and now I am happy to serve it to my own family & friends. It's real comfort food.

8-oz. pkg. wide egg noodles,
  uncooked and divided
1 to 2 t. butter, softened
2 lbs. ground beef
salt and pepper to taste

1/2 c. tomato sauce
1/4 lb. pasteurized process
  cheese spread, cubed
8-oz. pkg. shredded Cheddar
  cheese

Cook half of noodles according to package directions, reserving the remainder for another recipe. Drain; toss with butter and set aside. Meanwhile, brown beef in a skillet, adding salt and pepper. Drain. Add sauce and cheese spread to beef. Simmer until cheese starts to melt, stirring occasionally. Spread cooked noodles in the bottom of a lightly greased 2-1/2 quart casserole dish. Spread beef mixture evenly over noodles. Top with Cheddar cheese. Bake, uncovered, at 350 degrees until heated through and cheese is bubbly, about 15 minutes. Let stand for 5 minutes; cut into squares. Makes 6 servings.

Whimsical vintage aprons can be found easily at thrift shops and tag sales. Start your own collection to hang from pegs! Everyone can tie on their own ruffled, polka-dotted or flowered favorite whenever they help out in the kitchen.

Sloppy Joe Bake

Roberta Scheeler
Gooseberry Patch

A neat-to-eat version of an old standby.

2 c. biscuit baking mix	1 lb. ground beef
1/2 c. milk	15-1/2 oz. can Sloppy Joe sauce
2 T. butter, melted	4 slices American cheese,
1 egg, beaten	halved

Combine biscuit mix, milk, butter and egg together. Mix well; spread in the bottom and up the sides of a greased 9"x9" baking pan. Brown beef in a skillet and drain; add Sloppy Joe sauce and prepare as label directs. Spoon beef mixture evenly over batter. Bake, uncovered, at 400 degrees for 25 minutes. Arrange cheese on top and return to oven for 5 minutes, until cheese is melted. Makes 4 to 6 servings.

Give the same ol' mashed potatoes some pizazz...stir in
a tablespoon or two of horseradish sauce.

Emma's Ham & Broccoli Bake

Amy Blanchard
Clawson, MI

*My 8-year-old daughter loves this creamy, crunchy casserole...
need I say more?*

8-oz. pkg. elbow macaroni,
  cooked
10-oz. pkg. frozen chopped
  broccoli, thawed and drained
1-1/2 c. cooked ham, cubed
1-1/2 c. shredded Cheddar
  cheese, divided

1-1/2 c. French fried onions,
  divided
10-3/4 oz. can cream of
  celery soup
1 c. milk
1/4 t. garlic powder
1/4 t. pepper

In a large bowl, stir cooked macaroni, broccoli, ham, 3/4 cup cheese
and 3/4 cup onions together. Add remaining ingredients and mix
well. Pour mixture into a shallow 13"x9" baking pan that has been
sprayed with non-stick vegetable spray. Bake, uncovered, at
350 degrees for 30 minutes. Sprinkle remaining cheese and onions
on top. Bake for an additional 5 to 7 minutes, until cheese is melted.
Makes 4 servings.

Get a head start on dinner! Assemble a casserole
the night before, cover and refrigerate. Just add 15 to
20 minutes to the baking time...the casserole is ready
to serve when it's hot and bubbly in the center.

Chicken Spaghetti Deluxe

Dorothy Benson
Baton Rouge, LA

This recipe reminds me of cold winter days and Mom's warm kitchen with its inviting smells. It has a time-saving shortcut... the spaghetti doesn't need to be cooked first.

2 c. cooked chicken, chopped
8-oz. pkg. spaghetti, uncooked and broken up
1 c. celery, chopped
1 c. onion, chopped
1 c. yellow pepper, chopped

1 c. red pepper, chopped
2 10-3/4 oz. cans cream of mushroom soup
1 c. chicken broth
1/4 t. Cajun seasoning or pepper
1 c. shredded Cheddar cheese

Mix chicken, uncooked spaghetti and vegetables in a bowl. Whisk soup, broth and seasoning in a separate bowl. Add chicken mixture to soup mixture. Combine and transfer to a 13"x9" baking pan coated with non-stick vegetable spray. Sprinkle cheese over top. Cover with aluminum foil coated with non-stick vegetable spray. Bake at 350 degrees for 35 minutes. Uncover and bake for 10 more minutes. Makes 8 servings.

Create a clothesline-style gallery on a kitchen wall.
Tack up a few feet of rope or decorative braid, then use
old-fashioned clip clothespins to hang family photos
or the children's latest artwork.

109

Pork Chops Plus

Mare Hare
Marinette, WI

This was a recipe I gleaned from a German neighbor more than 20 years ago. It has a long German name that I've forgotten. I have made it many, many times since because it's quick, inexpensive and delish. Serve with a green veggie and buttered noodles...yum!

4 to 6 thick-cut smoked pork
   chops
garlic powder, salt and pepper
   to taste
4 to 6 thick slices sweet onion

8-oz. container sour cream
4 to 6 slices sharp Cheddar
   cheese
fresh tarragon to taste, chopped

Sprinkle pork chops with seasonings; arrange in a lightly greased shallow 13"x9" baking pan. Place a thick slice of onion on each chop, then a dollop of sour cream and a slice of cheese. Sprinkle with tarragon. Bake, uncovered, at 350 degrees for 15 minutes, until pork chops are heated through and onion is tender. Serves 4 to 6.

Garlicky Roasted Cauliflower

Lori Rosenberg
University Heights, OH

Even my picky eaters devour these cauliflowerets!

3 T. olive oil
2 T. garlic, minced
1 head cauliflower, cut into
   flowerets

salt and pepper to taste
1/3 c. grated Parmesan cheese
1 T. fresh parsley, chopped

Combine oil and garlic in a large plastic zipping bag. Add cauliflower; seal bag and shake to mix. Pour into a greased 2-quart casserole dish. Sprinkle with salt and pepper. Bake, uncovered, at 450 degrees for 25 minutes, stirring halfway through. Top with cheese and parsley. Broil for 3 to 5 minutes, until golden. Serves 6.

Chicken Superb

Diane Houser
Palm Harbor, FL

This scrumptious recipe is handed down from my grandmother,
who is now 97 years old. She is the family matriarch and
is an inspiration to us all.

3 lbs. boneless, skinless chicken
   breasts
garlic salt, paprika, salt and
   pepper to taste
3 T. butter, sliced

1 onion
3/4 c. apple jelly
1/2 c. cooking sherry or
   apple juice

Arrange chicken in a greased 13"x9" baking pan. Generously sprinkle
with seasonings; dot with butter. Using the fine side of a grater, grate
onion over chicken so that each piece is sprinkled with the juice.
Bake, uncovered, at 350 degrees for 45 minutes, or until tender.
Combine jelly and sherry or juice; mix well and pour over chicken.
Continue baking, uncovered, for one additional hour, basting
occasionally to glaze. Serves 6.

Indiana Hot Corn

Beth Garrison
Greenwood, IN

My mom would always try to get me to eat this homemade dish,
but I never would. But now as an adult, I love this recipe. The longer
it bakes, the spicier it gets!

28-oz. can diced tomatoes
2 15-oz. cans shoepeg corn
1 onion, minced

1 green pepper, chopped
3/4 t. cayenne pepper
1/2 c. butter, sliced

Pour undrained tomatoes and corn into a greased 2-1/2 quart
casserole dish. Stir in remaining ingredients except butter. Dot evenly
with butter; cover dish. Bake at 350 degrees for one to 1-1/2 hours,
stirring occasionally. Serves 6 to 8.

Gran Jan's Chicken Pie

Jan Morton
Hawkinsville, GA

This is a special favorite of my boys. It's easy to make if you start with a rotisserie chicken from the deli. It's delicious just the way it is, but add a drained can of mixed vegetables if you wish. Serve with steamed broccoli in cheese sauce.

4 c. cooked chicken, chopped
10-3/4 oz. can cream of chicken
  soup
1-1/2 c. chicken broth

2 T. cornstarch
1-1/2 c. self-rising flour
1 c. buttermilk
1/2 c. butter, melted

Place chicken in a 13"x9" baking pan coated with non-stick vegetable spray. Whisk together soup, broth and cornstarch; pour over chicken. Whisk together remaining ingredients; pour evenly over chicken mixture. Bake, uncovered, at 400 degrees for 40 minutes, or until golden. Serves 8 to 10.

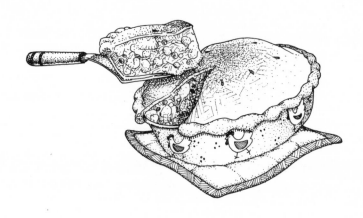

It's a lovely thing...everyone sitting down
together, sharing food.
-Alice May Brock

Favorite Tuna & Noodles

Crystal Hart
Dahlgren, IL

One taste and I feel like a kid again!

8-oz. pkg. medium egg noodles,
   uncooked
2 6-oz. cans tuna, drained
1-1/2 c. sour cream
3/4 c. milk
4-1/2 oz. can sliced mushrooms,
   drained

1-1/2 t. salt
1/4 t. pepper
1/4 c. dry bread crumbs
1/4 c. grated Parmesan cheese
2 T. butter, melted

Cook noodles as directed on package; drain. Return noodles to pan and stir in tuna, sour cream, milk, mushrooms, salt and pepper. Pour into an ungreased 2-quart casserole dish. Toss together remaining ingredients; sprinkle over casserole. Bake, uncovered, at 350 degrees for 35 to 40 minutes. Serves 4 to 6.

Share vacation memories by making placemats...fun for kids and for grownups too! Arrange snapshots, postcards, clippings, ticket stubs and other items on a sheet of scrapbooking paper. Glue in place, then add a protective sheet of clear self-stick plastic.

Lucas's Macaroni & Cheese

Ann Morris
Toledo, OH

Whenever my son makes this, it magically disappears...
macaroni & cheese is truly the best comfort food!

2 10-3/4 oz. cans Cheddar
  cheese soup
1 c. sour cream
16-oz. pkg. elbow macaroni,
  cooked

2 c. shredded Cheddar cheese
12 round buttery crackers,
  crushed
2 T. butter, melted

Mix soup and sour cream in a blender or by hand until well
blended. Toss cooked macaroni in soup mixture; spread in a buttered
13"x9" baking pan. Cover with cheese. Mix crushed crackers with
melted butter; sprinkle on top. Bake, uncovered, at 375 degrees for
20 minutes, until bubbly and golden. Serves 8.

Invite family & friends to an Unbirthday Party just for fun. Serve
everyone's favorite comfort foods, wear party hats, play games
like Pin the Tail on the Donkey and have a silly gift for each person
to unwrap. Everyone is sure to have a delightful time!

Jeannine's Noodle Casserole

Becky Kuchenbecker
Ravenna, OH

*My sister-in-law, Jeannine, makes this recipe for every family holiday.
I think you'll love it as much as we all do!*

16-oz. container cottage cheese
16-oz. container sour cream
1/2 c. butter, melted
2 eggs, beaten
1 t. salt

1/8 t. pepper
1/4 t. garlic powder
8-oz. pkg. thin egg noodles,
   cooked

Mix all ingredients except cooked noodles in a buttered 1-1/2 quart
casserole dish. Add noodles and stir well. Cover and bake at
300 degrees for 1-1/2 to 2 hours. Serves 8.

For an easy side dish alongside a casserole, arrange sliced fresh
veggies on a piece of aluminum foil. Top with seasoning salt
to taste, a sprinkle of dried herbs and two ice cubes. Fold the
foil to form a packet and bake at 450 degrees for
20 to 25 minutes. Scrumptious!

Pecan-Crusted Chicken

Denise Webb
Galveston, IN

This recipe was shared with my daughter, Amber, after the birth of her daughter, Karis. It is delicious...perfect for such a special occasion.

3 to 4 boneless, skinless
   chicken breasts
3 T. Dijon mustard
1 t. lemon juice

1/4 t. ground cumin
1/2 c. chopped pecans
1 T. dry bread crumbs
2 T. butter, melted

Place chicken breasts in a lightly greased 13"x9" baking pan. Mix together mustard, lemon juice and cumin; brush mixture over chicken. Toss together remaining ingredients; press mixture onto chicken. Bake, uncovered, at 375 degrees for 20 to 25 minutes, until chicken juices run clear when pierced. Makes 3 to 4 servings.

For a crispy, golden topping, leave the casserole dish
uncovered while it's baking.

Spiced Honey Chicken

Joan White
Malvern, PA

Delicious, easy to prepare and just a little exotic!

2 lbs. chicken thighs	nutmeg, salt and pepper to taste
1/4 c. honey	1/2 c. slivered almonds
1 clove garlic, minced	1/2 c. raisins
1 T. butter, melted	3 4-inch cinnamon sticks
3 T. lemon juice	cooked rice
1/2 t. lemon zest	

Arrange chicken thighs skin-side up in a lightly greased 2-quart casserole dish. Combine honey, garlic, butter, lemon juice and zest. Drizzle half of honey mixture over chicken. Sprinkle chicken with seasonings, almonds and raisins. Arrange cinnamon sticks evenly around casserole dish. Drizzle remaining honey mixture over chicken. Bake, covered, at 350 degrees for 45 minutes to one hour or until juices run clear, basting every 20 minutes. Discard cinnamon sticks; serve over cooked rice. Makes 3 to 4 servings.

For an old-fashioned treat, make your own butter. Pour a pint of heavy cream into a chilled wide-mouth jar, cap the jar tightly and take turns shaking until butter begins to form. When it's done, uncap the jar and rinse the butter lightly with cool water. Spread on warm, fresh-baked bread....delicious!

Loaded Cheeseburger Pie

Lauren Williams
Kewanee, MO

This is a dish that the whole family can agree on...there are never any leftovers when I serve it! Add a salad of chopped lettuce and tomatoes for a complete meal.

1 lb. ground beef
1 onion, chopped
1 green pepper, chopped
4 slices bacon, crisply cooked
  and crumbled
1/2 c. half-and-half

1/2 c. mayonnaise
8-oz. pkg. shredded Cheddar
  cheese
3 eggs, beaten
salt and pepper to taste

Brown beef, onion and pepper in a skillet. Drain; stir in bacon. Place in an ungreased shallow 8"x8" casserole dish or 9" deep-dish pie plate. Mix remaining ingredients until well combined; pour over beef mixture. Bake, uncovered, at 350 degrees for 45 minutes. Let stand for 5 to 10 minutes before slicing. Serves 4.

Monkey Taters

Lynn Fox
Gibsonburg, OH

I don't know where the funny name came from, but these potatoes are scrumptious!

32-oz. pkg. frozen potato puffs,
  partially thawed
Optional: 2 to 3 onions, chopped
10-3/4 oz. can cream of celery
  soup

16-oz. container sour cream
1/2 c. butter, melted
8-oz. pkg. shredded Cheddar
  cheese
Garnish: dried parsley

Mix all ingredients except parsley in a large bowl. Spoon into a greased 13"x9" baking pan. Sprinkle with parsley. Bake, uncovered, at 350 degrees for 45 to 60 minutes. Makes 8 to 10 servings.

Alice's Reuben Casserole

Chrys Pfahl
Bay Village, OH

My mom always took this to church suppers and people awaited its arrival eagerly. She never would share the recipe, but I've done so in her memory. Note that if there's caraway seed in the sauerkraut or the bread, you won't need to add any.

8 slices pumpernickel or rye bread, cubed and divided
14-1/2 oz. can sauerkraut, drained
12-oz. can corned beef, crumbled
1 c. sour cream
1 onion, finely chopped
1/2 t. dry mustard

Optional: 1 t. caraway seed, crushed
8-oz. pkg. shredded Monterey Jack cheese
8-oz. pkg. shredded Swiss cheese
1/2 c. butter, melted
Garnish: Thousand Island salad dressing

Spread half of bread cubes in the bottom of a 13"x9" baking pan that has been sprayed with non-stick vegetable spray. Layer on sauerkraut and corned beef. Mix sour cream, onion, mustard and caraway seed, if using; spread over corned beef layer. Layer on cheeses. Sprinkle top with remaining bread cubes and drizzle with butter. Bake, covered, at 350 degrees for 30 minutes. Serve warm, with salad dressing on the side. Makes 9 to 12 servings.

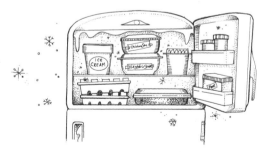

Team up! Invite your best girlfriend and prepare several casseroles together. Having someone to chat with makes prep time go quickly and when everything is done, you'll both have casseroles to freeze...a real time-saver.

Renae's Cheesy Shells

Renae Scheiderer
Beallsville, OH

With the rising price of groceries, I've been getting creative in the kitchen to make use of what I have on hand. This recipe was put together on a cold day to warm us up! It's good with a basket of warm crescent rolls and fresh spinach salad.

1 lb. ground beef, browned and
  drained
1 c. instant rice, cooked
1 c. spaghetti sauce
1 c. cottage cheese
1 t. garlic powder

1/4 t. salt
1 c. shredded Cheddar cheese,
  divided
12-oz. pkg. jumbo pasta shells,
  cooked

Combine all ingredients except shredded cheese and pasta shells in a large bowl. Add 1/2 cup shredded cheese and mix well. Spoon mixture into cooked shells. Arrange shells in a lightly greased 13"x9" baking pan; sprinkle with remaining shredded cheese. Bake, covered, at 350 degrees for 25 to 30 minutes. Serves 4 to 6.

Don't toss the wrapper after you've used a stick of butter. Instead, fold it up, place it in a plastic zipping bag and store it in the freezer. When it's time to butter a casserole dish, just take out a wrapper, let it soften slightly and use.

Tex-Mex Spaghetti Pie

Alice Folk
Butler, PA

A spicy southwestern version of everyone's favorite spaghetti pie.

8-oz. pkg. spaghetti, uncooked
1/2 c. milk
1 egg, beaten
1 lb. ground pork
1 onion, chopped
1 green pepper, chopped
1 clove garlic, chopped
1 T. chili powder

1/2 t. ground cumin
1/2 t. dried oregano
1/2 t. salt
1/4 t. pepper
15-oz. can tomato sauce
1 c. shredded Cheddar cheese
1 c. shredded Pepper Jack cheese

Cook spaghetti according to package directions; drain. Whisk together milk and egg; stir into hot spaghetti. Spread in a buttered 13"x9" baking pan. Meanwhile, cook pork, onion, green pepper and garlic together in a skillet over medium heat for about 6 minutes, until pork is browned. Drain; stir in seasonings and cook for 2 minutes. Stir in sauce and cook for 2 additional minutes. Spread sauce mixture over spaghetti. Sprinkle cheeses evenly over top. Set pan in lower third of oven. Bake, uncovered, at 425 degrees for about 10 minutes, until cheese is bubbly. Let stand about 5 minutes; cut into squares. Serves 4 to 6.

After a spicy meal, serve this easy, refreshing dessert. Dissolve a small 4-serving package of orange gelatin mix in one cup of boiling water. Slowly blend in 2 cups of softened vanilla ice cream. Spoon into 4 dessert dishes and chill for at least 20 minutes...yummy!

Baked Swiss Steak

Sharon Crider
Junction City, KS

A fix & forget main dish we all love...just add mashed potatoes.

2 lbs. beef round steak,
  1-inch thick
1 t. salt
1/4 t. pepper

1/2 c. onion, sliced
4-oz. can sliced mushrooms,
  drained
8-oz. can tomato sauce

Cut beef into serving-size pieces. Flatten with a meat mallet; sprinkle with salt and pepper and place in a lightly greased 13"x9" baking pan. Top with onion and mushrooms; pour sauce over all. Cover and bake at 350 degrees for 1-1/2 hours, basting occasionally with sauce. Uncover; bake 15 minutes longer. To serve, spoon sauce over beef. Serves 8.

Never-Fail Roast Potatoes

Debbie Issacson
Irvine, CA

These potatoes are irresistible, crisply golden and perfectly seasoned. My 17-year-old daughter finally gave them a try...now she loves them!

4 to 5 russet potatoes, cut into
  3/4-inch cubes
3 T. canola oil

seasoning salt, garlic powder
  and paprika to taste

In a large bowl, drizzle potatoes with oil and mix well. Shake seasonings over potatoes; mix very well and add more seasonings. Place potatoes in a single layer on a baking sheet that has been sprayed with non-stick vegetable spray. Shake seasonings over potatoes again. Bake, uncovered, at 350 degrees for 30 minutes. Turn potatoes over; bake for an additional 20 minutes. Turn potatoes again; return to oven for another 10 to 20 minutes, until desired crispness is reached. Makes 4 to 6 servings.

Best-Ever, Must-Have Meatloaf

Mary Jackson
Fishers, IN

Even the choosiest kids will love this recipe...the secret is the topping!

2 lbs. ground beef	1 c. catsup, divided
1.35-oz. pkg. onion soup mix	6 T. brown sugar, packed
1 c. soft bread crumbs	1 t. dry mustard
1 egg, beaten	Optional: 1/4 t. nutmeg

Mix beef, soup mix, bread crumbs, egg and 1/2 cup catsup in a bowl.
Form into a loaf; place in an ungreased 9"x5" loaf pan. Mix remaining
catsup, brown sugar, mustard and nutmeg, if using. Spoon over
meatloaf. Bake, uncovered, at 350 degrees for one hour. Serves 6 to 8.

Grandma Jeanette's Mashed Potatoes

Paula Kane
Grand Blanc, MI

No one made better mashed potatoes than Grandma!

8 potatoes, peeled and cooked	1/4 c. sour cream
8-oz. pkg. cream cheese, cubed	salt and pepper to taste
and softened	Garnish: melted butter, paprika

Mash potatoes while still warm; mix in cream cheese, sour cream, salt
and pepper. Spoon into a buttered 2-quart casserole dish. Brush with
melted butter and sprinkle with paprika. Bake, uncovered, at 350
degrees for 30 minutes, or until golden. Makes 4 to 6 servings.

Keep a bunch of fresh parsley fresh until ready to use...
tuck it into a water-filled tumbler in the fridge.

Ruth's Swiss Chicken

Ruth Thorpe
Langeloth, PA

*The most requested dish at every family gathering...I usually
have to make a double recipe!*

4 c. cooked chicken, cubed
10 slices bread, toasted and torn
   into small pieces
2 c. shredded Swiss cheese
1 c. celery, chopped
1/2 c. onion, diced

10-3/4 oz. can cream of celery
   soup
1/2 c. mayonnaise-type salad
   dressing
1/4 c. milk
1 t. salt

Mix all ingredients together and transfer to a lightly greased
13"x9" baking pan. Cover and bake at 350 degrees for 40 minutes.
Bake, uncovered, for an additional 10 minutes, or until golden and
heated through. Serves 4 to 6.

When delivering a yummy casserole to a new mom or neighbor,
add a potholder with the recipe tucked into the pocket.
So thoughtful!

Mom's Hamburger Hot Dish

Janelle Johnson
Clayton, WI

When I was growing up, this was the only hot dish Mom ever made, so it never had a name other than Hot Dish. I've made it my own with a couple of additions...it is always well liked.

1 lb. ground beef
1 onion, diced
1 c. celery, diced
1-1/4 c. chow mein noodles
10-3/4 oz. can chicken noodle
   soup
10-3/4 oz. can cream of
   mushroom soup

1-1/4 c. water
2 c. carrots, peeled, sliced and
   cooked
1/4 c. quick-cooking barley,
   uncooked

Brown beef, onion and celery in a skillet over medium heat; drain. Stir in remaining ingredients. Spoon into a lightly greased 3-quart casserole dish. Cover; bake at 350 degrees for 30 minutes. Uncover; bake an additional 30 minutes. Serves 4 to 6.

Bake a panful of roasted vegetables alongside a casserole. Slice, cube or trim zucchini, cauliflower, sweet peppers, mushrooms, asparagus and other veggies of your choice. Toss with olive oil and spread on a jelly-roll pan. Bake at 350 degrees for 30 to 35 minutes, stirring occasionally, until tender.

Herbed Chicken Dinner

Jennifer Kann
Dayton, OH

Real old-fashioned country goodness! Try it with fresh herbs when they're available...use 2 to 3 times the measurement of the dried herbs.

4 chicken breasts
4 baking potatoes, quartered
8-oz. pkg. sliced mushrooms
1/4 c. butter, melted
6 T. olive oil
2 T. onion, minced
2 cloves garlic, pressed

1/4 t. hot pepper sauce
2 t. dried thyme
1 t. dried rosemary
1/2 t. ground sage
1/2 t. dried marjoram
1 t. salt
1 t. pepper

Place chicken, potatoes and mushrooms in a large bowl; set aside. Whisk together remaining ingredients in a small bowl. Pour over chicken mixture; coat well. Remove chicken with tongs and place skin-side up in an ungreased shallow 13"x9" baking pan. Gently spoon potatoes and mushrooms over chicken, arranging in a single layer; drizzle with herb mixture. Cover and bake at 425 degrees for 35 to 45 minutes, until chicken juices run clear. Baste every 8 to 10 minutes with pan drippings; uncover during the last 7 to 10 minutes to lightly brown chicken. Arrange chicken and vegetables on a platter. Drizzle with some of the drippings before serving. Serves 4.

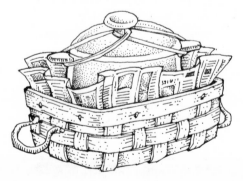

Hearty casseroles are super take-alongs for potlucks and pitch-in dinners. Keep them warm and yummy by wrapping the dish in aluminum foil and then tucking into a newspaper-lined basket.

Roast Chicken Meal-in-a-Pan

Sharon Velenosi
Stanton, CA

Just put this in the oven and forget it until it's time to serve. This dish even makes its own gravy, so have some crusty bread ready!

3 to 4 lbs. chicken
salt and pepper to taste
3 potatoes, peeled and quartered
3 onions, quartered
4 carrots, peeled and thickly
   sliced

2 zucchini, thickly sliced
15-oz. can green beans, drained
   and liquid reserved
10-3/4 oz. can tomato soup

Remove skin from chicken pieces; place chicken pieces in an ungreased large roasting pan. Sprinkle with salt and pepper. Arrange potatoes, onions and carrots between chicken pieces. Top chicken with zucchini, beans and soup. Pour reserved liquid from beans into pan. Cover and bake at 350 degrees for one hour and 45 minutes. Makes 4 to 6 servings.

Round out an easy one-dish dinner with a super-simple dessert. In parfait glasses, layer cubes of pound cake with thawed frozen peach slices and creamy whipped topping. Yummy!

Seven Seas Casserole

Mary Meek
Toledo, OH

I have been making this recipe for more than 35 years. It's always been a good standby...the ingredients are usually in my pantry and you don't even have to precook the rice or thaw the peas.

10-3/4 oz. can cream of
    mushroom soup
1-1/3 c. water
1/4 c. onion, chopped
1 t. lemon juice
1/4 t. salt

1/8 t. pepper
1-1/3 c. instant rice, uncooked
10-oz. pkg. frozen peas
5-oz. can tuna, drained
1/2 c. shredded Cheddar cheese

Combine soup, water, onion, lemon juice and seasonings in a saucepan; stir to blend. Bring to a boil over medium heat, stirring occasionally. Spoon half of mixture into a greased 1-1/2 quart casserole dish. Layer with uncooked rice, peas and tuna. Pour remaining soup mixture over all. Sprinkle with cheese. Cover and bake at 375 degrees for 10 minutes. Uncover and stir. Cover again; continue baking another 10 to 15 minutes, or until rice is tender. Let stand for 5 minutes before serving. Serves 4.

A tropical-themed dinner is a sure cure for chilly-weather cabin fever. Scatter seashells and sand dollars on the table and twine dollar-store flower leis around the place settings... or the diners!

Hawaiian Sausage Casserole

Linda Schaefer
Brownsville, TX

This is a pretty dish and tasty as well. You'll love the buttery brown sugar glaze.

20-oz. can pineapple chunks,
   drained and juice reserved
18-oz. can sweet potatoes,
   drained and sliced
12-oz. pkg. smoked pork
   sausage, sliced

3 T. brown sugar, packed
2 T. cornstarch
Optional: 1/4 t. salt
1 T. butter

Arrange pineapple chunks, sweet potatoes and sausage in a lightly greased 10"x6" baking pan. Combine reserved pineapple juice with enough water to equal 1-1/4 cups; set aside. In a saucepan, combine remaining ingredients. Gradually blend in reserved juice mixture. Cook and stir until thickened and bubbly; cook and stir for one more minute. Remove from heat; stir in butter. Pour over mixture in pan. Cover and bake at 350 degrees for 35 to 40 minutes, or until heated through. Makes 4 to 6 servings.

In search of a few new dinner ideas? Host a recipe swap party! Invite friends to bring a favorite casserole along with enough recipe cards for each guest. While everyone enjoys the delicious potluck food, collect the recipe cards, staple together and hand out when it's time to depart.

Clean-Your-Plate Casserole

Martha Brock
Sugar Land, TX

My family thinks this casserole tastes even better as leftovers!

1 lb. ground beef
16-oz. can stewed tomatoes,
  drained
8-oz. can tomato sauce
2 t. sugar
2 t. salt
1/4 t. pepper
1/4 t. garlic powder

1 c. sour cream
3-oz. pkg. cream cheese,
  softened
3/4 c. green onions, chopped
8-oz. pkg. fine egg noodles,
  cooked
1-1/2 c. shredded Cheddar
  cheese

Brown beef in a skillet over medium heat; drain. Stir in tomatoes, sauce, sugar and seasonings; heat through. In a small bowl, blend together sour cream, cream cheese and onions until smooth; add to beef mixture and mix well. Spread cooked noodles in a greased 10"x10" baking pan. Add beef mixture; top with cheese. Bake, uncovered, at 350 degrees for 30 minutes, or until hot and cheese is melted. Makes 4 to 6 servings.

A drizzle of chocolate makes homebaked cookies extra special. (Shhh...storebought cookies too!) Place chocolate chips in a small zipping bag and microwave briefly on high until melted. Snip off a tiny corner and squeeze to drizzle the chocolate...afterwards, just toss away the bag.

Marilyn's Sunday Casserole

Marilyn Pafford
Waco, TX

My husband loves this dish. The chicken is so tender and all the delicious flavors melt down to the potatoes. I like to put this casserole in the oven before church...when I return home, everything except dessert is ready to serve!

4 potatoes, peeled and thinly
   sliced
dried, minced onion to taste
garlic salt and seasoned salt to
   taste
6 slices American cheese
1 to 2 14-1/2 oz. cans green
   beans, drained

4 frozen boneless, skinless
   chicken breasts
26-oz. can cream of chicken or
   mushroom soup
1 c. milk

Spray a 13"x9" baking pan with non-stick vegetable spray. Layer sliced potatoes in pan; sprinkle with onion and seasonings. Layer with cheese slices and beans; place frozen chicken breasts on top. Blend soup and milk; pour over chicken. Cover pan with aluminum foil. Bake at 325 degrees for 3 hours. May also be baked at 375 degrees for 1-1/2 hours. Serves 4.

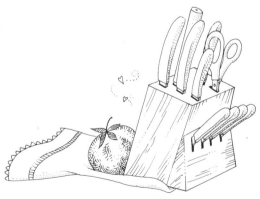

To test for doneness, insert the tip of a table knife in the center of a casserole. If the knife tip is hot to the touch when pulled out, the casserole should be heated through.

Quick & Easy Chicken Pot Pie

Susan Edsall
Alton, IL

I came up with this recipe one night when I had a rotisserie chicken and didn't want to just serve it heated up. Now whenever my husband sees a rotisserie chicken in the fridge, he asks hopefully, "Are we having that chicken pie again?" Enjoy with your favorite tossed salad and a fruit cup for dessert.

2 T. canola oil
20-oz. pkg. refrigerated diced
  potatoes with onion
16-oz. pkg. frozen mixed
  vegetables, thawed
10-3/4 oz. can cream of
  celery soup

10-3/4 oz. can cream of
  mushroom soup
2 T. salt-free herb seasoning
1/2 c. shredded 3-cheese blend
4-lb. deli roast chicken, shredded
8-oz. tube refrigerated crescent
  rolls

Heat oil in a skillet over medium heat; add potatoes. Cover skillet and cook until potatoes are golden, turning occasionally. Drain. Blend vegetables, soups, seasoning and cheese in a large bowl. Add potatoes and chicken to soup mixture; stir well. Spoon into a 13"x9" baking pan that has been sprayed with non-stick vegetable spray. Unroll crescent rolls and arrange on top. Cover loosely with aluminum foil. Bake at 375 degrees for 40 minutes, until hot and bubbly. Remove foil and bake an additional 10 minutes, until crescents are golden. Serves 6 to 8.

Dress up a country-style pot pie with a fresh herb crust.
Simply place leaves of fresh sage, dill or marjoram on the unbaked crust and gently press in with a rolling pin.

Patty's Penne & Chicken

Patty Smith
Kendallville, IN

*One night I just started tossing together items from the pantry...
this dish was the yummy result! My husband loved it and now
it's a regular in our house.*

2 c. cooked chicken, cubed
10-3/4 oz. can cream of chicken
  soup
4-oz. can sliced mushrooms,
  drained

14-1/2 oz. can mixed
  vegetables, drained
8-oz. pkg. penne pasta, cooked
1 c. shredded Mexican-blend
  cheese

Combine all ingredients except cooked pasta and cheese; stir in pasta.
Place in a lightly greased 2-quart casserole dish. Bake, uncovered, at
350 degrees for 25 minutes, or until bubbly. Remove from oven; top
with cheese. Return to oven and bake another 5 minutes, or until
cheese is melted. Serves 4.

A crunchy crumb topping adds texture and flavor to casseroles.
Soft bread crumbs tossed with melted butter are the classic
crumb topping. Crushed tortilla chips, pretzels or
savory snack crackers are all tasty too.

Wild Rice Hot Dish

June Sabatinos
Billings, MT

*This hearty dish is requested at every church social and there's never
any left to take home! Garnish it with a dollop of sour cream,
a sprinkle of slivered almonds or fresh parsley.*

2 lbs. ground beef round
1/2 c. butter
1 lb. sliced mushrooms
1 c. onion, chopped
1/2 c. celery, chopped
2 c. sour cream

1/4 c. soy sauce
2 t. salt
1/4 t. pepper
2 c. wild rice, cooked
1/2 c. slivered almonds

Brown beef in a skillet; drain and set aside. Melt butter in same skillet;
sauté mushrooms, onion and celery for 5 to 10 minutes. In a large bowl,
combine sour cream, soy sauce, salt and pepper. Stir in beef, mushroom
mixture, cooked rice and almonds. Toss lightly. Place mixture in a
buttered 3-quart casserole dish. Bake, uncovered, at 350 degrees for
about one hour, until heated through. Stir occasionally, adding a little
water if needed. Makes 12 to 16 servings.

Make a table tent to announce what you've brought to the potluck.
Glue a sweet fabric yo-yo or two to a folded card, write the
casserole name on the card and set it beside the dish.

Pioneer Beef Stew

Angie O'Keefe
Soddy Daisy, TN

There's nothing more satisfying than a hearty bowl of beef stew! Since it's baked, not simmered on the stovetop, this stew can be made while you do other things around the house.

14-1/2 oz. can petite diced
   tomatoes
1 c. water
3 T. quick-cooking tapioca,
   uncooked
2 t. sugar
1-1/2 t. salt

1/2 t. pepper
1-1/2 lbs. stew beef, cubed
3 to 4 potatoes, peeled and
   cubed
4 carrots, peeled and thickly
   sliced
1 onion, diced

In a large bowl, combine tomatoes with juice, water, tapioca, sugar, salt and pepper. Mix well; stir in remaining ingredients. Pour into a greased 3-quart casserole dish. Cover and bake at 375 degrees for 1-1/2 to 2 hours, until beef and vegetables are tender. Serves 4 to 6.

Served with warm homebaked biscuits, any casserole is a down-home delight. They're easy to make with biscuit baking mix. Just follow the package directions, but here's a secret... for the flakiest biscuits, don't overwork the dough. Simply stir to mix and roll or pat out gently.

Curly Pasta Bake

Jean DePerna
Fairport, NY

This recipe was given to me by a girlfriend nearly 20 years ago. After a busy day, it's a convenient meal the whole family enjoys. It's also an excellent dish to take to potlucks.

1 lb. ground beef
1 onion, chopped
1 green pepper, chopped
10-3/4 oz. can golden
   mushroom or cream of
   mushroom soup

8-oz. can tomato sauce
1-1/2 c. shredded Cheddar
   cheese, divided
1/2 t. salt
8-oz. pkg. rotini pasta, cooked

In a large skillet over medium heat, brown beef, onion and green pepper together; drain. Add soup, sauce, one cup cheese and salt. Stir in cooked pasta; transfer to a greased 2-1/2 quart casserole dish. Sprinkle with remaining cheese. Bake, uncovered, at 350 degrees for 30 minutes, or until bubbly. Makes 4 to 6 servings.

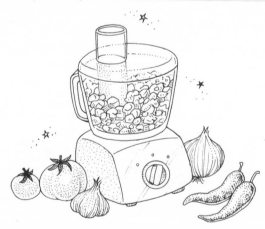

Mix up flavorful homemade salsa year 'round. Combine a 14-1/2 ounce can of diced tomatoes with green chiles, 1/2 cup diced onion, a minced garlic clove and a tablespoon of lime juice. Enjoy it chunky style, or for a smoother consistency, place in a food processor and pulse 2 to 3 times.

Deep-Dish Sausage Pizza

Kathleen Sturm
Corona, CA

Why go out to a pizza parlor, when you can feast on a hot, hearty pizza right from your own kitchen? It's chock-full of the great Italian sausage and sweet pepper flavors that we love.

16-oz. pkg. frozen bread dough,
  thawed
1 lb. sweet Italian pork sausage,
  casings removed
2 c. shredded mozzarella cheese
1 green pepper, cut into squares
1 red pepper, cut into squares

28-oz. can diced tomatoes,
  drained
3/4 t. dried oregano
1/2 t. salt
1/4 t. garlic powder
1/2 c. grated Parmesan cheese

Press thawed dough into the bottom and up the sides of a greased 13"x9" baking pan; set aside. In a large skillet, crumble sausage and cook until no longer pink; drain. Sprinkle sausage over dough; top with mozzarella cheese. In the same skillet, sauté peppers until slightly tender. Stir in tomatoes with juice and seasonings; spoon over pizza. Sprinkle with Parmesan cheese. Bake, uncovered, at 350 degrees for 25 to 35 minutes, until crust is golden. Makes 8 servings.

For the tastiest results, reduce the oven temperature by 25 degrees if you're using glass or dark metal baking pans... they retain heat more than shiny metal pans do.

Ben Getty Casserole

Whitley Sakas
Sequim, WA

During the Second World War, my parents were in the Air Force and food was limited. Colonel Ben Getty was one of my parents' best friends and he would bring over his family to share a double batch of this delicious casserole with our own family. It didn't have a name, so we named it after him. I hope you'll enjoy this dish as much as we have!

1 lb. lean ground beef or turkey
1/4 c. onion, chopped
Optional: 1/4 c. green pepper, chopped
salt and pepper to taste
7-oz. pkg. elbow macaroni, cooked

10-3/4 oz. can cream of mushroom soup
10-3/4 oz. can tomato soup
8-1/2 oz. can petite peas
6 slices pasteurized process cheese

In a large skillet over medium heat, brown beef or turkey with onion and green pepper, if using. Drain; add salt and pepper. Stir in cooked macaroni and soups; gently fold in undrained peas. Pour all into a lightly greased 13"x9" baking pan and cover. Bake at 350 degrees for 50 to 60 minutes, until bubbly. Uncover; arrange cheese slices on top and return to oven until melted, about 5 minutes. Serves 4 to 6.

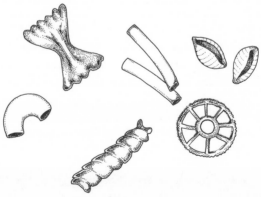

Pasta shapes like bowties, seashells and corkscrew-shaped cavatappi all work well in casseroles...why not give a favorite casserole a whole new look?

Fu-Man-Chew

*Ruie Richardson
Marinette, WI*

*Don't be confused by this recipe's funny name...it's just
good old chop suey!*

1 c. onions, chopped
2 T. oil
2 lbs. ground beef
1 c. celery, sliced
2 10-3/4 oz. cans cream of
  mushroom soup
1 c. instant rice, uncooked
16-oz. can bean sprouts,
  drained

6-oz. can sliced water chestnuts,
  drained
1/4 c. soy sauce
salt and pepper to taste
10-oz. pkg. frozen snow peas,
  partially thawed
3-oz. can chow mein noodles

In a skillet over medium heat, sauté onions in oil for 5 minutes. Add
beef and brown with onions; drain. Stir in remaining ingredients
except peas and noodles. Pour into a greased 3-quart casserole dish.
Bake, covered, at 350 degrees for 30 minutes. Stir in peas; top with
noodles. Bake, uncovered, for an additional 30 minutes. Serves 8.

A slick trick when you don't want to leave a favorite casserole
baking dish in the freezer! First, line it with aluminum foil,
bake your casserole, wrap and freeze. Then lift out your frozen
casserole and return the dish to the cupboard. Later, when you're
ready to enjoy your casserole, simply unwrap, place it
back into the same dish and bake.

Tallarine Casserole

Sue Roberson
Peoria, AZ

My mom used to serve this yummy casserole when I was growing up...
it has been in my family for over 40 years. Its name comes from
a Spanish word for noodles.

8-oz. pkg. wide egg noodles,
   uncooked and divided
1 lb. lean ground beef
1 onion, diced

2 10-3/4 oz. cans tomato soup
15-1/4 oz. can corn, drained
8-oz. pkg. shredded Cheddar
   cheese, divided

Measure out 2 cups noodles and cook according to package directions.
Reserve remaining noodles for another recipe. Brown beef and onion
in a skillet over medium heat; drain. Combine cooked noodles, beef
mixture, soup and corn in a greased 2-quart casserole dish; stir in
one cup cheese. Mix well and top with remaining cheese. Bake,
uncovered, at 350 degrees for 30 minutes, until bubbly. Serves 6.

Clean that casserole dish in a jiffy! Fill the empty dish with
hot, soapy water and let it soak while enjoying dessert...
no more scrubbing off baked-on food.

Layered Ravioli Florentine

Michelle Campen
Peoria, IL

This delicious, cheesy dish is similar to lasagna, but goes together quickly using frozen ravioli.

10-oz. pkg. frozen chopped
  spinach, thawed and drained
15-oz. container ricotta cheese
1 c. shredded mozzarella
  cheese, divided
1 c. shredded Parmesan cheese,
  divided

1 egg, beaten
1 t. Italian seasoning
16-oz. jar marinara sauce,
  divided
25-oz. pkg. frozen 4-cheese
  ravioli, divided

Combine spinach, ricotta cheese, 1/2 cup mozzarella cheese, 1/2 cup Parmesan cheese, egg and seasoning; set aside. Spread half of sauce in the bottom of a lightly greased 9"x9" baking pan. Arrange half of frozen ravioli in a single layer on top of sauce. Top with all of spinach mixture and remaining ravioli, sauce and mozzarella cheese. Bake, covered, at 400 degrees for 30 minutes. Remove from oven. Sprinkle with remaining Parmesan cheese; let stand about 15 minutes before serving. Serves 6.

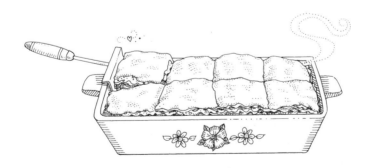

To avoid scratching non-stick baking pans, be sure to serve up casseroles using plastic or wood spatulas, never metal.

Marcia's Zesty Chicken Spaghetti

Sherry Duval
Avoca, IA

My sister-in-law shared this quick & tasty casserole recipe with me. For an extra flavor boost, add a couple of chicken bouillon cubes to the water when cooking the spaghetti.

4 c. cooked chicken, diced
7-oz. pkg. thin spaghetti, cooked
16-oz. pkg. pasteurized process
   cheese spread, cubed
1/2 c. sour cream
1/2 c. onion, diced

1/2 green pepper, diced
14-1/2 oz. can diced tomatoes
   with green chiles
8-1/2 oz. can petite peas,
   drained

Combine all ingredients together; mix well. Transfer to a greased 3-quart casserole dish. Bake, uncovered, at 350 degrees for 30 minutes, until heated through. Serves 6 to 8.

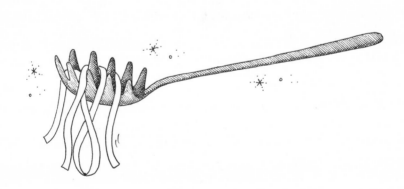

Most casseroles can be frozen for two to three months with little or no loss of flavor and texture. Be sure to label and date them before placing in the freezer.

One-Dish Dinners

Spicy Glazed Chicken & Barley

JoAnn

Looking for a new way to fix chicken? Try this tasty recipe...it stirs up in a jiffy and even comes with its own little side dish.

6 chicken thighs
2 T. soy sauce
2 t. honey
2 t. spicy brown mustard
14-1/2 oz. can chicken broth
   with roasted vegetables

3/4 c. quick-cooking barley,
   uncooked
1/2 c. frozen petite peas
salt and pepper to taste

Arrange chicken in a lightly greased 13"x9" baking pan. Whisk together soy sauce, honey and mustard; brush half of mixture over chicken. Bake, uncovered, at 375 degrees for 15 minutes. Turn chicken over; brush with remaining soy sauce mixture. Bake an additional 15 minutes, until chicken is golden and juices run clear. Meanwhile, bring broth to a boil in a saucepan. Stir in uncooked barley. Reduce heat; cover and simmer for 5 minutes. Add remaining ingredients to barley. Cook an additional 5 to 7 minutes, until barley is tender and liquid is absorbed. Serve chicken with barley on the side. Serves 3 to 4.

Hang a vintage wall-mounted magazine rack in the kitchen to store favorite cookbooks. Give it a fresh coat of paint in a fun color or enjoy it just as you found it.

Speedy Potato Puff Bake

Cynde Dupre
Windsor, CO

A variation on a biscuit-topped casserole, using something my kids ask for again & again...potato puffs! My husband loves this also and requests it often.

1 lb. ground beef
Optional: 1 onion, diced
10-3/4 oz. can cream of
  mushroom or chicken soup
14-1/2 oz. can green beans,
  drained

1 to 2 c. shredded Cheddar
  cheese
26-oz. pkg. extra crispy frozen
  potato puffs

In a skillet over medium heat, brown beef, adding onion if desired. Drain. Add soup and beans; stir until combined. Transfer to a greased 2-quart casserole dish. Pat mixture level with the back of a spoon and sprinkle with desired amount of cheese. Arrange potato puffs on top. Bake, uncovered, at 400 degrees until bubbly and puffs have cooked through, about 20 minutes. Serves 4 to 6.

Ingredient swaps are easy with most casserole recipes. If there's no cream of mushroom soup in the pantry, cream of celery or chicken is sure to be just as tasty... you may even discover a new way you like even better!

Easy Chicken Divan

Bethi Hendrickson
Danville, PA

Quick, tasty and economical. Try it with asparagus and Swiss cheese too...yum!

3 boneless, skinless chicken
   breasts, cooked and diced
10-oz. pkg. frozen chopped
   broccoli, cooked and drained
2 10-3/4 oz. cans cream of
   chicken soup

3/4 c. mayonnaise
1 t. lemon juice
1 c. shredded Cheddar cheese
1/2 c. Italian-flavored dry
   bread crumbs
1/4 c. butter, melted

Toss cooked chicken and broccoli together. Mix soup, mayonnaise and lemon juice; add to chicken mixture. Pour into a greased 13"x9" baking pan; top with cheese. Toss bread crumbs and butter together; sprinkle mixture over cheese. Bake, uncovered, at 350 degrees for 25 to 30 minutes. Serves 6 to 8.

Are your best girlfriends coming over for a ladies' luncheon? Add some sparkle to the table with thrift-shop treasures! Wrap beaded bracelets around the napkins...fasten an old-fashioned clip earring to each placecard. So pretty!

Zucchini Pasta Casserole

Lisa Langston
Walden, TX

You'll love this light, delicious dish that's packed with veggies! I have never seen this recipe anywhere else, so I'm happy to share it.

16-oz. pkg. linguine pasta,
   uncooked and divided
1/2 lb. lean ground beef
1 onion, chopped
1 green pepper, chopped
28-oz. can diced tomatoes

1 clove garlic, minced
1/2 t. dried oregano
3/4 lb. zucchini, sliced
Garnish: grated Parmesan
   cheese

Measure out a nickel-size bundle of pasta; reserve the remainder for another use. Cook pasta just until tender, according to package directions; drain. Meanwhile, in a skillet over medium heat, brown beef; drain. Stir in onion, pepper, tomatoes with juice, garlic and oregano. Cook until thickened. Arrange zucchini slices in a lightly greased shallow one-quart casserole dish. Cover with pasta, then beef mixture; sprinkle with cheese. Bake, uncovered, at 375 degrees for 25 minutes. Serves 4.

A crisp green salad goes well with all kinds of casseroles.
For a zippy citrus dressing, shake up 1/2 cup olive oil,
1/3 cup lemon or orange juice and a tablespoon of Dijon
mustard in a small jar and chill to blend.

Eggplant Parmigiana

Annette Mullan
North Arlington, NJ

Our favorite meatless meal! For a deliciously different serving suggestion, layer slices of warm baked eggplant on crusty Italian rolls for hero sandwiches.

2 eggplants, peeled and sliced
   into 1/4-inch rounds
1-1/2 c. all-purpose flour
2 eggs, beaten
1-1/2 c. dry bread crumbs
1-1/2 t. salt, divided
1/4 t. pepper, divided
1 clove garlic, halved

3/4 c. olive oil, divided
28-oz. can diced tomatoes
1/3 c. tomato paste
2 T. fresh basil, minced
1 c. grated Parmesan cheese
1/2 lb. mozzarella cheese, thinly
   sliced and divided

Dip eggplant slices into flour, then eggs, then into bread crumbs seasoned with 1/2 teaspoon salt and 1/8 teaspoon pepper. Place slices on a baking sheet; refrigerate for 20 minutes. In a saucepan, sauté garlic in 2 tablespoons oil for one to 2 minutes. Remove garlic from saucepan; add tomatoes with juice, tomato paste, basil and remaining salt and pepper. Cover; simmer over low heat for 30 minutes. Heat remaining oil in a skillet. Sauté eggplant on both sides until golden; drain on paper towels. Spread a thin layer of warm sauce mixture in a lightly greased 15"x10" jelly-roll pan. Alternately layer eggplant, remaining sauce, Parmesan and mozzarella cheeses. Bake, uncovered, at 350 degrees for 30 minutes. Makes 4 to 6 servings.

Make a handy potholder rack from a vintage wooden rolling pin. Place a row of cup hooks along one side and add a strip of homespun tied to each end for hanging. So simple!

Grandma Jane's Chinese Tuna Casserole

Karen Larkin
Blue Lake, CA

A real hand-me-down recipe! My mother used to make this dish when I was a child. I served it to my boys when they were small and now they both make it for their families. Try it with turkey too!

3 c. chow mein noodles, divided
10-3/4 oz. can cream of mushroom soup
2 6-oz. cans tuna, drained and flaked
1 c. cashew pieces
1 c. celery, chopped
8-oz. can sliced water chestnuts, drained
1/4 c. bean sprouts, drained
1/4 c. chopped red or green pepper
1/4 c. shredded Monterey Jack cheese
1/4 c. green onion, chopped
1/2 c. milk
1 T. soy sauce

Combine 2 cups noodles with remaining ingredients in a buttered 2-quart casserole dish. Mix well. Sprinkle remaining noodles over the top. Bake, uncovered, at 350 degrees for 30 minutes, or until bubbly in the center. Serves 6.

Create a cozy corner for yourself with a comfy chair and a small table. With a casserole baking in the oven, you'll have a quiet place to read a book, write in a journal or just enjoy a catnap before dinner.

Speedy Skillets

Skillet Swiss Steak

Charlene McCain
Bakersfield, CA

My mother was a real expert on comfort food. She served her Swiss steak with homemade mashed potatoes, simmered green beans and warm-from-the-oven biscuits with butter and honey. Yum!

2 lbs. beef round steak, cut into
  serving-size pieces
salt and pepper to taste
1/4 c. all-purpose flour

1 T. oil
1 onion, sliced into rings
15-oz. can tomato sauce

Pound beef with a meat mallet to tenderize. Sprinkle with salt and pepper; lightly flour on both sides. Heat oil in a skillet over medium heat. Brown beef on both sides over medium heat. Add onion to skillet underneath beef. Pour sauce over beef; cover skillet. Turn heat to low and simmer for 25 to 30 minutes, or until beef is cooked through and onion is tender. Serve beef topped with tomato gravy and onion from skillet. Serves 6 to 8.

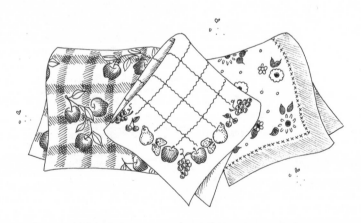

Search out yard sales or auctions for vintage tablecloths and tea towels with brightly colored fruit motifs...they'll add a dash of nostalgia to any meal.

Creamed Beef over Biscuits

Staci Meyers
Montezuma, GA

*I was raised on this delicious recipe. It cooks up quickly
from just a few simple ingredients...try it!*

1 lb. ground beef
1/4 c. butter
12-oz. can evaporated milk,
  divided

1 T. all-purpose flour
salt and pepper to taste
10-oz. tube refrigerated biscuits,
  baked and split

Brown beef in a skillet; drain. Add butter and one cup milk to skillet.
Simmer over medium heat until butter is melted. Combine remaining
milk with flour. Mix well until smooth; pour over beef mixture in
skillet. Add salt and pepper; stir well. Reduce heat to medium-low
and simmer for 3 to 5 minutes, until thickened. Serve over split
biscuits. Serves 4.

Season an old cast-iron skillet to make it practically non-stick...
it's easy. Brush a thin coat of canola oil or shortening all over
the skillet and bake it at 300 degrees for one hour. Then
turn off the heat and let the skillet cool completely in
the oven...that's all it takes!

Sizzling Potato Skillet

Kim Allmon
Chesterton, IN

One of my favorite go-to dishes when time is short and I don't want to clean more than one pan. For variety, use a scalloped potato mix instead of the au gratin mix.

1 lb. Kielbasa turkey sausage, halved and sliced 1/2-inch thick
Optional: 1 T. water or oil
5-1/4 oz. pkg. au gratin potato mix
2-1/2 c. water

8-oz. pkg. frozen California-blend vegetables, thawed
1 to 2 c. shredded Cheddar cheese
Garnish: 1/4 c. French fried onions

Brown sausage in a skillet over medium heat, adding a tablespoon of water or oil if desired to prevent sticking. Add potato mix and water to skillet; do not follow package instructions. Cover and cook over medium heat for about 20 minutes, or until potatoes are almost tender, stirring occasionally. Add vegetables; cover and continue cooking an additional 10 minutes, until potatoes are tender and vegetables are heated through. Remove from heat and sprinkle with cheese. Cover and let stand until cheese is melted. Top with onions just before before serving. Makes 4 servings.

Lots of skillet recipes call for chopped onion, green pepper or celery. Whenever you're slicing & dicing enough for one meal, take a moment to chop some extra veggies for later in the week and tuck them away in the fridge. What a time-saver!

Smoked Sausage Stir-Fry

Diane Cohen
The Woodlands, TX

This veggie-packed dish stirs up in no time at all...you'll love it!

2 T. olive oil
14-oz. pkg. smoked pork
    sausage, thinly sliced
16-oz. pkg. frozen Asian-blend
    stir-fry vegetables

6 T. sweet-and-sour sauce
cooked rice

In a skillet, heat oil over medium-high heat. Add sausage; sauté for one minute. Add vegetables; cook and stir for 6 to 8 minutes, or until thawed and heated through. Stir in sauce; cook and stir for one additional minute, until coated. Serve over hot cooked rice. Serves 6.

For a tasty change from rice, serve a stir-fried dish spooned over quick-cooking thin spaghetti or a bed of no-cooking-needed crispy chow mein noodles.

Speedy Chicken Cacciatore

Angela Murphy
Tempe, AZ

My family loves this classic Italian dish because it's yummy...I love it because it's so quick to fix. I like to serve it with quick-cooking angel hair pasta. Pass the Parmesan cheese, please!

4 boneless, skinless chicken
  breasts
2 T. olive oil
1 c. sliced mushrooms
Optional: 1 c. green pepper,
  sliced

14-1/2 oz. can diced tomatoes
6-oz. can tomato paste with
  basil, garlic and oregano
2/3 c. water
salt and pepper to taste

In a skillet over medium-high heat, cook chicken in oil until golden, about 3 to 4 minutes per side. Remove chicken from skillet; set aside. Add mushrooms and green pepper, if using, to skillet. Cook, stirring occasionally, until tender, about 4 minutes. Stir in tomatoes with juice, tomato paste and water. Add salt and pepper as desired. Return chicken to skillet; spoon sauce over chicken. Cover and simmer until chicken juices run clear, about 15 minutes. Serves 4.

Inexpensive light olive oil is just fine for frying. Save the extra-virgin olive oil for making salad dressings, where its delicate flavor can be enjoyed.

Spicy Chicken Tenders

Danielle Fish
Acworth, GA

One night I created this dish for my husband, Ryan, and he ate his dinner so fast, he was asking for seconds! I serve it with roasted broccoli and cauliflower for a complete meal.

3/4 lb. boneless chicken tenders
1 T. olive oil
Optional: 1 c. sliced mushrooms

3 T. reduced-sodium soy sauce
1 to 1-1/2 t. red pepper flakes
cooked rice

In a skillet over medium-high heat, cook chicken in oil until golden. Stir in remaining ingredients except rice, adding red pepper flakes to taste. Let simmer until chicken is cooked through. Serve over cooked rice. Makes 2 to 3 servings.

A refreshing beverage for a spicy stir-fry supper!
Combine equal amounts of ginger ale and pineapple juice.
Pour into ice-filled tumblers and garnish with fresh
fruit slices stacked up on drinking straws.

Yummie Drummies

Barb Traxler
Mankato, MN

Eating chicken drumsticks makes you feel like a kid again! I like to serve these with baked potatoes and homemade coleslaw.

1/2 c. chicken broth
1/3 c. oil
1/4 c. green onions, chopped
1/4 c. fresh parsley, basil or
   cilantro, chopped

2 t. sugar
1/2 t. salt
1/2 t. pepper
10 chicken drumsticks

Combine all ingredients except chicken in a gallon-size plastic zipping bag. Add chicken; seal bag and refrigerate for 3 to 4 hours. Drain, discarding marinade. Cook chicken in a frying pan over medium-high until almost done, about 10 minutes. Finish by grilling for about 10 minutes over medium heat. Serves 5.

Fried Squash & Potatoes

Ann Mathis
Biscoe, AR

My friend, Judy, gave me this recipe. She says she cannot cook, but boy, is this good and easy! I usually use an electric skillet for this recipe, but it can also be cooked in a skillet on the stovetop.

2 to 3 t. oil
3 yellow squash, sliced
3 potatoes, sliced

1/3 to 1/2 c. onion, chopped
1/3 c. all-purpose flour

Heat oil in a skillet over medium heat; add vegetables. Sprinkle flour over vegetable mixture and stir to lightly coat vegetables. Cook, stirring frequently, until tender and lightly golden. Serves 6.

Pork Chops Piquante

Joan White
Malvern, PA

One of the very best pork recipes I've ever tasted! The pork chops are very tender and the sauce is scrumptious. Country-style pork ribs can also be prepared this way.

4 bone-in pork chops
salt and pepper to taste
2 T. oil

1/2 c. chicken broth
1/2 c. apricot preserves
2 T. Dijon mustard

Sprinkle pork chops with salt and pepper. Heat oil over medium-high heat in a skillet. Add pork chops; cook for 3 minutes on each side. Drain; transfer pork chops to a 13"x9" baking pan sprayed with non-stick vegetable spray. Bake at 350 degrees for 10 minutes. While pork chops are baking, add broth to skillet. Bring to a boil and cook down to half, about 5 minutes. Add preserves and bring back to a boil. Cook, stirring until thick and syrupy. Stir in mustard; lower heat to medium. Return pork chops to skillet; turn to coat. Spoon remaining sauce over pork chops. Makes 4 servings.

Pork chops, chicken breasts and cubed stew beef will brown better if patted dry first with a paper towel.

Cheesy Chicken & Rotini

Diane Cohen
The Woodlands, TX

A delicious made-from-scratch meal...with no more effort than preparing a boxed dinner helper!

16-oz. pkg. rotini pasta, divided and uncooked
1 lb. boneless, skinless chicken breasts, cut into bite-size pieces

1 green pepper, thinly sliced
16-oz. jar spaghetti sauce
8-oz. pkg. shredded Italian-blend or mozzarella cheese, divided

Cook 2 cups rotini according to package directions; drain. Save remaining pasta for another use. Spray a skillet with non-stick vegetable spray; heat over medium-high heat. Add chicken; cook and stir for 5 minutes. Add pepper and cook for an additional 5 minutes, until chicken is cooked through. Stir in sauce, cooked rotini and one cup cheese; sprinkle with remaining cheese. Remove from heat; cover and let stand for one to 2 minutes, until cheese is melted. Makes 5 servings.

Hot dog and hamburger buns make the yummiest garlic bread. Spread bun halves with softened butter, add garlic salt to taste and pop under the broiler until toasty and golden.

Just 5 Ingredients!

Rachel's Pizza Pasta Skillet

Rachel Boreing
Culleoka, TN

A super-simple recipe I created one night...my husband told me it was a "keeper" and I have been making it regularly ever since!

16-oz. pkg. penne rigate pasta, uncooked and divided
1 lb. ground pork sausage
16-oz. jar spaghetti sauce
Garnish: grated Parmesan cheese

Cook half the pasta according to package directions; drain. Save remaining pasta for another use. Brown sausage in a skillet over medium heat; drain. Add sauce and cooked pasta to skillet. Stir and heat about 5 minutes, until warmed. Top with cheese. Serves 4.

Zucchini Parmesan

Cathy Elgin
Saint Louis Park, MN

A really tasty way to use a garden bounty of zucchini.

1/2 to 1 t. garlic, minced
1 T. olive oil
4 zucchini, thinly sliced
14-1/2 oz. can Italian-seasoned diced tomatoes
1 t. seasoned salt
1/4 t. pepper
Garnish: grated Parmesan cheese

In a skillet over medium heat, sauté garlic in oil. Add zucchini; cook and stir for 4 to 5 minutes, until crisp-tender. Stir in tomatoes with juice, salt and pepper. Simmer for 9 to 10 minutes, until liquid is absorbed and mixture is heated through. Serve with a slotted spoon; sprinkle with Parmesan cheese. Serves 6.

A sweet china saucer that has lost its teacup makes a useful spoon rest on the stovetop.

Country-Style Taters

Lorrie Smith
Drummonds, TN

An old family favorite...at home alongside pork chops, baked chicken, scrambled eggs or whatever you like.

2 T. oil
5 to 6 russet potatoes, peeled
    and cubed

1 onion, chopped
1 green pepper, diced
salt and pepper to taste

Heat oil in a large skillet over medium heat. Add potatoes, onion and green pepper. Cover; cook until potatoes are tender and lightly golden. Add salt and pepper to taste. Serves 4.

Chile Sweet Corn

Rita Morgan
Pueblo, CO

We enjoy this fresh-tasting side dish year 'round.

1 bunch green onions, sliced
3 T. olive oil
20-oz. pkg. frozen corn, thawed
    and drained

4-oz. can diced green chiles
salt and pepper to taste

In a skillet over medium heat, sauté onions in oil for 2 minutes. Stir in remaining ingredients. Cook until vegetables are tender and heated through. Makes 4 servings.

Plant a vegetable garden with the kids...picky eaters are sure to be willing to sample veggies that they grew themselves! Some easy-to-grow favorites are carrots, radishes, sweet peas, green beans and all kinds of peppers.

Sesame-Asparagus Sauté

Valerie L'Arrivee
Alberta, Canada

Fresh asparagus is such a treat...this savory recipe
makes it even tastier!

1 bunch asparagus, trimmed
  and chopped
1 t. oil

1 clove garlic, chopped
salt and pepper to taste
1 t. sesame seed

Cover asparagus with water in a saucepan. Boil for 5 minutes; drain.
Heat oil in a skillet over medium heat. Add asparagus and remaining
ingredients. Sauté for several minutes, until tender. Serves 4.

Brown Sugar-Basil Carrots

Charlene Boice
Lake City, FL

A great way to get your kids to eat carrots! Handed down from my
step-grandmother, who passed away several years ago.

5 T. butter, divided
1 lb. carrots, peeled and thinly
  sliced
3 T. fresh basil, chopped and
  divided

1/4 c. brown sugar, packed
1/2 t. salt

Melt 4 tablespoons butter in a skillet over low heat. Add carrots
and one tablespoon basil; cover and simmer until carrots are almost
tender. Stir in brown sugar and salt; add remaining butter and basil to
taste. Cook, stirring frequently, until carrots are tender and ingredients
have all blended together. Serves 4.

A generous square of red-checkered homespun makes a
cozy liner for a basket of hot rolls.

Mom's Stovetop Macaroni

Shannon James
Georgetown, KY

With four kids in elementary school, we try to stay on a budget. This meal is great for summertime because I don't have to turn on my oven. It sounds simple but is so tasty!

16-oz. pkg. elbow macaroni,
   uncooked
6 slices bread, torn and finely
   crumbed

2 cloves garlic, chopped
3 T. olive oil, divided

Cook macaroni according to package directions; drain and keep warm. Combine crumbs, garlic and one tablespoon oil in a skillet. Cook over medium heat until crumbs are lightly toasted. Add crumb mixture and remaining oil to macaroni; toss to mix. Serves 6.

Grandma's Wilted Greens

Robin Hill
Rochester, NY

I remember my grandmother fixing all kinds of garden greens this way... mustard greens, Swiss chard, even dandelion leaves. Be sure to pat the rinsed leaves really dry, so the skillet doesn't spatter.

1 T. olive oil
2 cloves garlic, pressed
Optional: 1/8 t. red pepper
   flakes

1-1/2 lbs. spinach, trimmed
   and torn
1/4 t. salt

Heat oil in a skillet over medium-high heat. Add garlic and cook for one minute, until golden. Add red pepper flakes, if using; cook 30 seconds. Add greens to skillet; sprinkle with salt. Cook, stirring constantly, for 3 to 5 minutes, until greens are wilted. Serves 4.

Pepperoni & Noodles

Marlene Mock
Eugene, OR

One of my son's favorites...he still requests it when he comes home for a visit. Add chopped green pepper or tomato for a change.

1 c. pepperoni slices
1 c. onion, chopped
8-oz. pkg. spaghetti, cooked
3/4 to 1 c. shredded mozzarella
   cheese

Optional: grated Parmesan
   cheese

Place pepperoni and onion in a skillet over medium heat. Cook until pepperoni edges start to curl and onion is tender. Toss mixture with cooked spaghetti; add mozzarella cheese and toss again. Sprinkle with grated Parmesan cheese, if desired. Serves 4.

Add the words "Today's Menu" across the top of a small blackboard with acrylic paint. Hang it in the kitchen and update it daily with chalk...everyone is sure to hurry to the dinner table when they know what's for dinner!

Grandma's Meal-in-a-Pot

Dianna Brock
Tonawanda, NY

When my grandmother passed away, my grandfather gave me this
recipe of hers. It's a hearty, filling side dish to serve with your
choice of meat like grilled Polish sausage or ham steak.

16-oz. pkg. bowtie pasta,
  uncooked
1 head cabbage, cored and
  quartered

1/2 c. butter
1 onion, diced
salt and pepper to taste

Cook pasta according to package directions; drain and keep warm.
Cover cabbage with water in a saucepan; boil until tender. Melt butter
in a skillet over medium heat; sauté onion. When cabbage is cooked,
drain and cut into small pieces. Add cabbage and pasta to onion in
skillet. Stir in salt and pepper. Toss to mix well. Serves 6.

While the main dish simmers, turn leftover mashed potatoes
into twice-baked potatoes. Stir in minced onion, crumbled bacon,
sour cream and shredded cheese to taste. Pat into mini casserole
dishes. Bake at 350 degrees until hot and golden...scrumptious!

Smoky Mountain Skillet

Ginger Marshall
Louisville, TN

Many nights at our family cabin, my mom would make this easy dish that we all loved. I can still see us all now, sitting around that big round oak table, eating this dish with wedges of warm cornbread and ripe red homegrown tomatoes...what a delicious memory!

1/4 c. oil
5 to 6 potatoes, peeled or
   unpeeled, cubed
1 onion, chopped

salt and pepper to taste
12-oz. can roast beef in gravy
1/2 c. water

Heat oil in a skillet; add potatoes, onion, salt and pepper. Cook over medium heat until potatoes are tender and golden. Add roast beef in gravy and mix in well; stir in water. Cover skillet and cook over low heat for 15 to 20 minutes. Serves 5 to 6.

Take the family out to dinner...at a nearby park! While a simple skillet meal simmers on the grill, everyone can swing on the swings, play croquet or just enjoy the sights and sounds of nature. Afterwards, make homemade ice cream or s'mores for dessert. What fun!

Daddy's Goulash

Nicole Brock
Kirklin, IN

A super recipe for family nights...when supper is as quick and yummy as this, we have more time to enjoy together!

2 lbs. ground beef
10-3/4 oz. can nacho cheese
  soup
10-3/4 oz. can tomato soup

1/2 c. plus 2 T. water
13-1/2 oz. pkg. nacho-flavored
  tortilla chips

Brown beef in a skillet over medium heat; drain. Stir in soups and water. Heat through, stirring occasionally. To serve, place a handful of crushed tortilla chips into each soup bowl. Ladle 1/2 cup of beef mixture over chips. Serves 8.

A Lazy Susan is oh-so handy for keeping canned soups,
vegetables and other pantry staples at your fingertips.
Just give it a quick spin to bring the item you need
to the front of the cupboard.

Beef Patties in Mushroom Gravy

Barbara Waddell
Wichita Falls, TX

I came up with this quick & easy dish years ago...it's still one of my now-grown sons' favorites! Serve it with mashed potatoes for a delicious homestyle meal.

4 lean ground beef patties
salt and pepper to taste
10-3/4 oz. can cream of
 mushroom soup

1-1/4 c. milk

Heat a skillet over medium-high heat. Add beef patties; sprinkle with salt and pepper. Brown patties on both sides; reduce heat to low. Mix soup and milk in a bowl; slowly pour soup mixture into skillet. Cook, stirring occasionally, until gravy thickens and patties are cooked through. Serves 4.

Peppery New Potatoes

Denise Mainville
Huber Heights, OH

A quick & flavorful way to enjoy the little spuds.

1-1/2 T. olive oil
2 lbs. new redskin potatoes,
 quartered

1/2 t. red pepper flakes
salt and pepper to taste

Heat oil in a frying pan over very high heat. Carefully add potatoes. Reduce heat to medium-high; cook potatoes, turning often, until evenly golden. Sprinkle with red pepper flakes; cover and cook until tender, about 10 minutes. Add salt and pepper as desired. Makes 4 servings.

Save bacon drippings in an empty jar or container kept in the fridge. Add just a little to the oil when frying potatoes for delicious country-style flavor.

Smoky Cabbage

Jean Tonkin
Sydney, Australia

I made this up when we were not long married and there were only a few things in the fridge. Fifty years later, we still enjoy it as a favorite supper!

1 onion, chopped
1 to 2 T. butter
1 head cabbage, cored and
   coarsely chopped

6 smoked frankfurters or
   sausages, sliced
2 to 3 potatoes, peeled, cubed
   and cooked

In a large frying pan over medium heat, cook onion in butter until transparent. Add cabbage; cook and stir until it turns bright green and crisp-tender. Add frankfurters or sausages and potatoes. Stir until heated through and edges of cabbage begin to turn golden. Serves 4.

Southern Fried Apples

Kristine Marumoto
Sandy, UT

Serve these with pork chops or grilled sausage...make them even yummier with a dollop of whipped cream!

1/4 c. shortening
6 tart apples, cored, peeled and
   sliced
1 t. lemon juice

1/4 c. brown sugar, packed
1/8 t. salt
Garnish: apple pie spice

Melt shortening in a skillet over medium heat. Add apples evenly in a single layer. Sprinkle with lemon juice, brown sugar and salt. Cover; cook over low heat for 15 minutes, until apples are tender and juicy. Sprinkle with spice and serve warm. Serves about 6.

Protect a favorite cookbook from cooking spatters...slip the opened book into a large plastic zipping bag before you begin.

Herbed Butter Noodles

Shelley Turner
Boise, ID

A vendor at our local farmers' market shared this recipe with me when she sold me some fresh herbs...it's delightful! Try other fresh herbs like savory, chervil, thyme and oregano too.

12-oz. pkg. wide egg noodles,
   uncooked
2 T. butter
1/4 c. fresh parsley, minced

1 t. fresh rosemary, minced
1/2 t. salt
1/4 t. pepper

Cook noodles as package directs; drain and keep warm. Place remaining ingredients in a skillet over low heat. Stir until butter melts and mixture is well blended. Add noodles to skillet; toss to coat well. Serve immediately. Serves 6.

Bake up some sweet and tangy cranberry muffins for dinner! Just stir dried cranberries and a little orange zest into a cornbread muffin mix. Bake as directed on the package... serve topped with a pat of butter. Yum!

Beefy Taco Skillet

Jessica Robertson
Fishers, IN

A Mexican dinner-in-a-pan, pronto! Stir in some yellow corn
and black beans for extra color and flavor.

1 lb. ground beef
10-3/4 oz. can tomato soup
1 c. chunky salsa
1/2 c. water

8 10-inch flour tortillas, cut
  into 1-inch squares
1 c. shredded Cheddar cheese,
  divided

Brown beef in a skillet over medium heat; drain. Stir in remaining ingredients except cheese; add 1/2 cup cheese. Bring to a boil. Reduce heat to low; cover and cook for 5 minutes. Top with remaining cheese before serving. Serves 4.

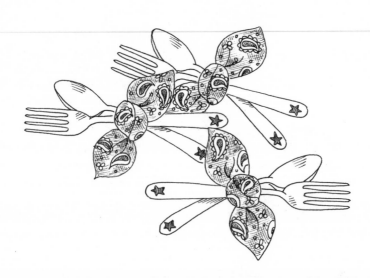

Give tonight's table a little flair...knot a cheery bandanna around each set of flatware. Bandannas come in so many bright colors, everyone can choose their own favorite.

Bacon Cheeseburger Pasta

Nichole Martelli
Santa Fe, TX

Hearty and satisfying...we all love it!

8-oz. pkg. rotini pasta,
    uncooked
1 lb. ground beef

6 slices bacon, diced
10-3/4 oz. can tomato soup
1 c. shredded Cheddar cheese

Cook pasta according to package directions; drain and keep warm. In a skillet, brown beef over medium heat; drain and set aside. In same skillet, cook bacon until crisp; remove to paper towels with a slotted spoon. Discard drippings; add pasta to same skillet. Stir in soup, beef and bacon; heat through. Sprinkle with cheese. Cover and heat until cheese is melted. Makes 4 to 6 servings.

Bacon continues to cook briefly even after it's removed from heat. To avoid burning, be sure to remove it from the skillet just before it reaches the desired crispness.

Easy Chicken Fettuccine

Ashley Jones
Greenville, OH

*I am 23 years old and have loved **Gooseberry Patch** cookbooks for
5 years now. My mother and I have nearly all of them. Recently I tried
this for the first time...it's delicious and ready in 20 minutes! People
keep asking me for the recipe and I am happy to share.*

8-oz. pkg. cream cheese, cubed
3/4 c. grated Parmesan cheese
1/2 c. butter, sliced
1/2 c. milk
1 lb. boneless, skinless chicken
    breasts, cubed

1 T. oil
12-oz. pkg. fettuccine pasta,
    cooked

Combine cheeses, butter and milk in a saucepan. Stir continuously
over medium heat until cheeses melt and mixture is smooth; keep
warm. In a large, deep skillet over medium-high heat, cook chicken in
oil until juices run clear; drain. Add cooked pasta to skillet and top
with cheese sauce; toss to mix well. Serves 6.

Invite your friends and neighbors to a good old-fashioned block
party. Set up picnic tables, arrange lots of chairs in the shade and
invite everyone to bring a favorite dish. Whether it's a summer
cookout or a fall harvest party, you'll make some
wonderful memories together!

Denise's Penne Rosa

*Denise Webb
Galveston, IN*

*Creamy and delicious...this recipe always makes me feel like
I'm eating at my favorite Italian restaurant!*

1 T. butter
1 T. garlic, minced
14-1/2 oz. can whole tomatoes,
  finely chopped, drained and
  1/4 c. juice reserved
1 t. dried basil

salt and pepper to taste
2/3 c. whipping cream
8-oz. pkg. penne rigate pasta,
  cooked
Garnish: 2 T. grated Parmesan
  cheese

Melt butter in a skillet over medium heat. Add garlic and cook for one
minute, until golden. Add tomatoes with reserved juice, basil, salt and
pepper; heat to boiling. Reduce heat; simmer for 5 minutes, or until
most of liquid is reduced. Stir in cream. Heat through on low heat for
one minute, or until thickened. Toss sauce with cooked pasta; sprinkle
with cheese. Serve immediately. Serves 4.

If a favorite non-stick skillet has gotten sticky, here's a simple
solution. Fill it with one cup water, 1/2 cup vinegar and
2 tablespoons baking soda. Bring to a boil for a few minutes.
Rinse well with hot water and wipe clean...no more stickiness!

Chicken à la King

Beth Bundy
Long Prairie, MN

Real comfort food, yet it cooks up in a jiffy! Serve this over buttered toast points or split warm biscuits.

8-oz. can sliced mushrooms, drained and 1/4 c. liquid reserved
1/2 c. onion, chopped
1/2 c. butter, sliced
1/2 c. all-purpose flour

2 c. half-and-half
1-3/4 c. chicken broth
2 13-oz. cans chicken breast, drained
1/2 t. salt
1/4 t. pepper

In a skillet over medium heat, cook mushrooms and onion in butter for 5 minutes. Slowly add flour; cook and stir until simmering. Stir in half-and-half, broth and reserved mushroom liquid. Heat to boiling over low heat, stirring constantly. Add chicken, salt and pepper; cook until hot and bubbly. Makes 4 servings.

Throw an apron party! Invite your best girlfriends to tie on their frilliest vintage aprons and join you in the kitchen to whip up a favorite dish together. It's a fun way to catch up with everyone while enjoying some yummy food.

Speedy Salmon Sauce

Louise Graybiel
Ontario, Canada

One day I was planning to make a tuna casserole, but when I opened the cupboard, I realized I had canned salmon and cream of asparagus soup, not tuna and cream of mushroom. So I just tossed then together... it was delicious!

10-3/4 oz. can cream of asparagus soup	1 T. lemon juice
1/2 c. milk	7-1/2 oz. can salmon, drained and flaked
1/2 c. mayonnaise	4 puff pastry shells, baked

Combine soup and milk in a skillet over medium heat; stir until smooth and just bubbly. Add mayonnaise and lemon juice; blend well. Stir in salmon and heat through. To serve, spoon into pastry shells. Serves 4.

Make crunchy toast cups to fill with a favorite saucy skillet dish. Trim the crusts off bread slices, flatten slightly and brush both sides with melted butter. Gently press the slices into ungreased muffin cups. Bake at 350 degrees for 15 to 20 minutes, until toasty and golden.

Busy-Day Lasagna Toss

Cathy Forbes
Hutchinson, KS

This recipe is super when your family's begging for lasagna and you don't have time for all the layering. It's a big hit with my teens and hubby...and makes plenty for leftovers the next day!

1 lb. ground beef
1 c. green pepper, chopped
1/2 c. onion, chopped
3 cloves garlic, minced
26-oz. jar spaghetti sauce
1-2/3 c. water

1/4 c. Italian salad dressing
1/4 c. brown sugar, packed
12 oven-ready lasagna noodles,
  broken into quarters
Optional: 1/2 c. ricotta cheese
1 c. shredded mozzarella cheese

Brown meat in a large, deep skillet over medium heat; drain. Add pepper, onion and garlic; sauté until tender. Mix in sauce, water, salad dressing and brown sugar; bring to a boil. Stir in noodles; reduce heat to medium-low. Cover and cook, stirring occasionally, until noodles are tender, about 10 to 15 minutes. Remove from heat. Stir in ricotta cheese, if using. Sprinkle with mozzarella cheese; cover. Let stand for 5 minutes, or until cheese is melted. Serves 6.

Sun-ripened tomatoes are such a treat! Serve them up with just a dash of oil & vinegar, a pinch of salt and a toss of chopped fresh basil. When garden tomatoes aren't in season, try roma tomatoes...they're available year 'round.

Quick Skillet Spaghetti

Lisa Parrish
Trinity, NC

My husband requests this recipe for dinner weekly! It's so easy because you don't even have to boil water for the spaghetti. Try it with half sausage and half ground turkey too.

1 lb. sweet Italian ground
  pork sausage
1 clove garlic, pressed
7-oz. pkg. spaghetti, uncooked
  and broken into 1-inch
  lengths
2 14-oz. cans diced Italian
  tomatoes

15-oz. can tomato sauce
1 T. fresh parsley, chopped
2 t. dried basil
3 T. shredded Italian-blend
  cheese

In a skillet over medium heat, brown sausage for about 5 to 7 minutes, stirring often. Drain; stir in garlic and broken spaghetti. Cook for 5 minutes, stirring often. Add remaining ingredients except cheese and stir until well blended. Heat to boiling. Reduce heat to low; cover and simmer about 20 minutes, until spaghetti is tender. Sprinkle with cheese. Cover and cook for 2 to 3 minutes longer to melt cheese. Serves 4 to 6.

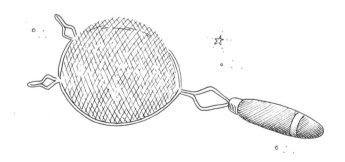

Save time on clean-up...be sure to use a spatter screen when frying. If there's no spatter screen handy, try inverting a kitchen sieve over the skillet.

Simple & Hearty Burritos

Wendy Hayden
Lexington, KY

I came up with this recipe when our refrigerator went out and I had to use what I had on hand in the kitchen. It was a success!

1 lb. ground beef or Italian
   ground pork sausage
15-oz. can favorite chili
16-oz. can refried beans
2 to 4 T. taco seasoning mix

8 10-inch flour tortillas
Garnish: shredded cheese,
   chopped tomato, chopped
   onion, shredded lettuce,
   sour cream, salsa

Brown beef or sausage in a skillet over medium heat; drain. Add chili, beans and desired amount taco seasoning to skillet. Mix well. Cook until hot and bubbly. Fill tortillas with mixture; add any desired toppings and roll into burritos. Serves 6 to 8.

Rosalee's Salsa Rice

Rosalee Varady
Spring City, PA

My husband loves this recipe so much, I have to double it for him! Choose salsa that's as mild or spicy as you prefer.

1-1/2 c. water
1 c. salsa
2 cubes chicken bouillon

1 T. paprika
2 c. instant rice, uncooked

Combine water, salsa, bouillon and paprika in a skillet. Bring to a boil over medium-high heat. Remove from heat; stir in rice. Cover and let stand 6 minutes. Fluff with a fork before serving. Serves 4.

For cornbread with a crisp, golden crust, bake it in
a vintage sectioned cast-iron skillet.

Mexican Skillet Spaghetti

Betty Lou Wright
Hendersonville, TN

When my husband and I were first married, this tasty recipe was a favorite of ours. Quick & easy to prepare, it was perfect since I had little cooking experience. Over the years I forgot about it, but recently rediscovered it in an old cookbook. Now that we're retired, we're enjoying this tasty reminder of our younger days.

1 lb. ground beef chuck
15-oz. can tomato sauce
3 c. plus 2 T. water
2 1-1/4 oz. pkgs. taco
   seasoning mix

2 T. onion, minced
8-oz. pkg. spaghetti, uncooked
   and broken up
1/2 c. shredded Cheddar cheese

Brown beef in a skillet over medium heat; drain. Stir in sauce, water, seasoning mix and onion. Bring to a boil; reduce heat and simmer, covered, until spaghetti is tender, about 25 to 30 minutes. Sprinkle with cheese; let stand until cheese melts. Serves 4 to 6.

A dollop of homemade guacamole jazzes up any south-of-the-border meal. Slice a couple of ripe avocados, scoop them into a bowl and mash with a fork to the desired consistency. Stir in 1/2 cup of your favorite salsa, a teaspoon of lime or lemon juice and a dash of salt...yum!

Country Fried Pork Chops

Gladys Pilch
Sylva, NC

These pork chops are so easy to fix, no wonder they're a favorite of mine! I serve them over buttered egg noodles, followed by hot cinnamon applesauce and cookies for dessert.

4 pork chops
4-oz. can sliced mushrooms, drained
1/2 to 1 T. shortening
10-3/4-oz. can cream of celery soup

1/2 c. water
1/4 t. dried thyme
6 pearl onions
1 c. carrots, peeled and sliced

In a skillet over medium-high heat, brown pork chops and mushrooms in shortening. Drain; stir in soup, water and thyme. Add onions and carrots. Cover and cook over low heat for 45 minutes, or until tender. Stir occasionally. Serves 4.

Whipped sweet potatoes are yummy with pork or chicken. Drain a 32-ounce can of sweet potatoes and add 2 tablespoons orange juice, one tablespoon brown sugar and one tablespoon melted butter. Beat until smooth. Spoon into a greased casserole dish and bake at 350 degrees until hot, about 15 minutes.

So-Easy Pork Fritters

Elena Nelson
Concordia, MO

This is my husband's favorite meal. I created this recipe to mimic a menu item at our favorite restaurant when we were dating. That restaurant has been out of business for years, but this recipe always takes us back to those good old days. These fritters are excellent in a sandwich too.

1 lb. pork tenderloin, sliced
   1/2-inch thick
1 egg, beaten
3 T. milk
1 sleeve saltine crackers,
   finely crushed

3/4 c. all-purpose flour
1 t. salt
1/2 t. pepper
oil for frying

Tenderize pork slices with a meat mallet; set aside. Place egg and milk into a small bowl and blend well. Combine cracker crumbs, flour and seasonings in another bowl. Dip pork slices first into egg mixture, then into crumb mixture. Press in crumb mixture to coat very well. Heat 1/2 inch of oil in a skillet over medium-high heat. Add pork slices; fry until deep golden on both sides, turning as needed. Serves 4.

Skillet gravy is super-easy to make. Melt a tablespoon of butter in a skillet over medium heat, then sprinkle in a tablespoon of all-purpose flour and whisk for one minute. Add a can of chicken or beef broth and a dash of pepper. Stir well, lower heat and simmer for about 5 minutes, until gravy is thickened.

Saucy Dogs

Kristin Santangelo-Winterhoff
North Chili, NY

My grandparents have been making this recipe for years. It is a fast, easy dish that really dresses up a hot dog...the best! Make sure to have some nice crusty bread and a crisp green tossed salad waiting nearby... heavenly!

1 green pepper, thinly sliced
1 red pepper, thinly sliced
1 onion, thinly sliced
1 clove garlic, cut in thirds
salt and pepper to taste

1/2 c. olive oil
8 to 12 hot dogs, sliced into
   1-inch pieces
29-oz. can tomato purée or
   crushed tomatoes

Place peppers, onion and garlic in a deep skillet. Add salt and pepper to taste. Pour in oil; sauté over medium heat until lightly golden. Add hot dogs to skillet; sauté until golden. Stir in purée or tomatoes. Reduce heat and simmer for about 30 minutes. Serves 4.

To clean a cast-iron skillet, simply scrub with coarse salt,
wipe with a soft sponge, rinse and pat dry. Salt cleans cast iron
thoroughly without damaging the seasoning as
dish detergent would.

Inside-Out Stuffed Pepper

Charlene McCain
Bakersfield, CA

*A quick and tasty dish for those nights when you get home late
from work and everybody's hungry.*

1 green pepper, top removed	1-1/2 c. cooked rice
1 lb. ground beef	8-oz. can tomato sauce
1 onion, chopped	salt and pepper to taste

Bring a saucepan of salted water to a boil. Add green pepper and cook for 8 to 10 minutes, until tender. Drain; cool slightly and slice pepper into strips. Meanwhile, cook beef and onion in a skillet over medium heat, stirring often, until beef is browned and onion is translucent. Drain; add green pepper and cooked rice to skillet. Pour tomato sauce over skillet mixture; stir and heat through. Add salt and pepper to taste. Serves 4.

Whip up a new tablecloth or runner and matching napkins from cotton fabric...no sewing needed! Cut fabric to size, fold over a narrow hem and press it in place with double-faced iron-on bonding tape.

Denise's Shrimp Pasta

Denise Thom
Lake George, NY

I made this up when I was a stay-at-home mom 23 years ago...
we still enjoy it. Add a fresh tomato salad and a basket of
hot garlic bread...scrumptious!

16-oz. pkg. frozen medium
  shrimp, thawed
8-oz. bottle Italian salad
  dressing
2 cloves garlic, pressed
16-oz. pkg. angel hair pasta,
  uncooked

2 T. olive oil
1 tomato, diced
1 onion, chopped
1 T. fresh basil, chopped
1 t. pepper

Place shrimp in a bowl with salad dressing and garlic. Toss to coat; let stand for about 30 minutes. Cook pasta according to package directions. Drain; place in a serving bowl and keep warm. Heat oil in a small frying pan; sauté tomato and onion until translucent. Top pasta with shrimp mixture, tomato mixture, basil and pepper. Mix gently and serve warm. Serves 4.

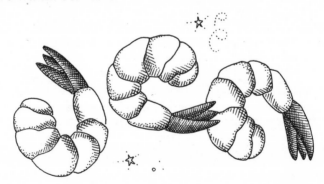

Start a supper club with friends...choose a recipe theme each time,
divide up the menu, then get together to cook and eat the meal.
You'll have a ball and everyone will come away with
some tasty new dinner ideas.

Sole in Dill Butter

Evelyn Love
Standish, ME

Serve with steamed broccoli for a quick & easy light meal.

1/4 c. butter, softened
1 t. dill weed
1/2 t. onion powder
1/2 t. garlic powder
Optional: 1/2 t. salt

1/4 t. white pepper
2 lbs. sole fillets
Garnish: additional dill weed,
  lemon wedges

Blend butter and seasonings in a small bowl. Transfer to a cast-iron skillet; heat over medium heat until melted. Add fish fillets to skillet. Sauté for several minutes on each side, until fish flakes easily with a fork. Serve with desired garnishes. Serves 6.

Armenian Rice Pilaf

Lori Rosenberg
University Heights, OH

A speedy side that will add pizazz to any ordinary meal...using just four items you probably already have on hand!

1/2 c. butter
8-oz. pkg. wide egg noodles,
  uncooked

10-1/2 oz. can chicken broth
2 c. long-cooking rice, uncooked

Melt butter in a heavy skillet or saucepan. Add uncooked noodles; cook and stir until lightly golden. Add broth and uncooked rice; bring to a full boil. Lower heat and simmer, covered, for 20 minutes, until noodles and rice are tender. Makes 4 to 6 servings.

Protect non-stick skillets from scratching when stacked...tuck a coffee filter or paper plate in between them.

Company Chicken

Lacey Purcell
Littleton, CO

A family favorite. This dish is made in just one pan, takes only about 20 minutes, and most important...it's scrumptious!

4 to 6 boneless, skinless
   chicken breasts
1 T. oil
1 c. sour cream
10-3/4 oz. can cream of
   mushroom soup

4-oz. can sliced mushrooms,
   drained
1.35-oz. pkg. onion soup mix
1 T. lemon juice
1 T. dill weed
Optional: cooked rice

Place chicken and oil in a large skillet over medium-high heat. Cook until chicken is golden on both sides. Add remaining ingredients except rice, mixing well. Bring to a boil; reduce heat. Cover and simmer until chicken juices run clear. Serve chicken over cooked rice, if desired; top with sauce from skillet. Serves 4 to 6.

friends ♥ forever

The better part of one's life consists of one's friendships.
~Abraham Lincoln

Ranch Chicken & Noodles

Bev Fisher
Mesa, AZ

*Most people like chicken and will enjoy this recipe as much as I do.
When I serve it to company, they always ask for the recipe.*

6 slices bacon, cut into narrow
strips
4 boneless, skinless chicken
breasts, cut into bite-size
pieces
2 T. all-purpose flour

2 T. ranch salad dressing mix
1-1/4 c. milk
8-oz. pkg. medium egg noodles,
cooked
Garnish: grated Parmesan
cheese

In a skillet over medium heat, cook bacon until crisp. Drain bacon on
paper towels; reserve 2 tablespoons drippings in skillet. Cook chicken
in reserved drippings until tender and golden on all sides. Sprinkle
flour and dressing mix over chicken in skillet; stir in milk. Cook and
stir until thickened and bubbly. Cook and stir for one minute more.
Stir in bacon. Serve chicken and sauce over cooked noodles, sprinkled
with cheese. Serves 4.

The easiest-ever way to cook egg noodles...bring a big pot of water
to a rolling boil, then add the noodles. Remove from heat, cover
and let stand for 20 minutes, stirring twice. Perfect!

Scalloped Cabbage & Ham

Katie Wollgast
Florissant, MO

Packaged coleslaw mix makes this old-fashioned favorite easy...
horseradish gives it a little kick! Add a basket of warm pumpernickel
bread for a hearty, satisfying meal.

2 c. cooked ham, cubed
1/2 c. long-cooking rice,
   uncooked
1 onion, chopped
1 T. oil
10-3/4 oz. can cream of
   mushroom soup

1-1/2 c. milk
1 t. prepared horseradish
1 t. salt
16-oz. pkg. coleslaw mix
Garnish: 1 T. dried parsley

In a skillet over medium heat, sauté ham, uncooked rice and onion
in oil until lightly golden. Stir in remaining ingredients except parsley;
bring to a boil. Reduce heat to low; cover and simmer for 20 to
25 minutes, stirring occasionally, until rice and coleslaw mix are
tender. Sprinkle with parsley just before serving. Serves 4.

Chicken Dinners

Lots of recipes start with cooked and cubed chicken breasts.
Save time and money...buy chicken in bulk and roast or simmer it
all at once. When cooled, pack recipe-size portions of chicken
in freezer bags and freeze. They'll thaw quickly when
you're ready to use them.

Basil Broccoli Pasta

Denise Bliss
Milton, NY

This can either be a yummy side or a meatless main. Broccoli is our favorite vegetable, but feel free to add any veggie you like.

6 T. olive oil
2 T. butter
4 cloves garlic, sliced
1 bunch broccoli, sliced into
  flowerets
1 c. chicken broth

16-oz. pkg. rigatoni pasta,
  cooked
2 T. fresh basil, chopped
pepper to taste
Optional: grated Parmesan
  cheese

Heat oil and butter in a skillet or large saucepan over medium heat. Add garlic; cook until lightly golden. Add broccoli to pan; increase heat. Cook and stir gently until broccoli is almost tender, 3 to 4 minutes. Add broth; reduce heat and simmer until broccoli is tender. Add cooked pasta to skillet; mix thoroughly to allow pasta to absorb flavor. Transfer to a serving dish; top with remaining ingredients. Serves 4.

For a tasty change from bread & butter, serve slices of warm French or Italian bread with dipping oil. Pour a thin layer of extra-virgin olive oil into saucers, drizzle with a little balsamic vinegar and sprinkle with dried oregano. Scrumptious!

Cube Steak in Savory Gravy

Deborah Burns
Lebanon, OR

An easy meal that's perfect on a chilly evening. Serve with fluffy mashed potatoes and tender green beans.

1 lb. beef cube steak, cut into
    4 serving-size pieces
1/4 c. all-purpose flour
1 onion, chopped
1 T. oil
1 c. water

1/4 c. catsup
1 T. Worcestershire sauce
1 t. beef bouillon granules
1/2 t. Italian seasoning
1 t. salt
1/4 t. pepper

Coat beef pieces with flour; set aside. In a skillet over medium heat, sauté onion in oil until translucent. Add beef and brown on both sides; drain. Mix remaining ingredients in a small bowl; pour over beef mixture. Heat until boiling; reduce heat. Cover and simmer until beef is tender, about 1-1/4 to 1-1/2 hours. Serves 4.

Bake a shortcake for dessert to fill with strawberries or peaches.
Mix up 2-1/3 cups biscuit baking mix, 3 tablespoons sugar,
1/2 cup milk and 3 tablespoons melted margarine. Pat into an
ungreased 9" round cake pan. Bake at 350 degrees until golden,
10 to 12 minutes. Split while still warm, layer with fruit and
whipped cream and cut into wedges...mmm!

Southern Succotash

Zoe Bennett
Columbia, SC

*Try this with the kernels sliced from several ears of
sweet corn too...yum!*

2 slices bacon, chopped
1 onion, chopped
1 stalk celery, diced
10-oz. pkg. frozen corn, thawed
10-oz. pkg. frozen baby lima
    beans, thawed

1/4 c. chicken broth
1/2 t. salt
1/8 t. pepper
Optional: fresh chives, snipped

In a skillet over medium heat, cook bacon until crisp. Remove bacon to
a paper towel; set aside. Add onion and celery to drippings in skillet;
cook and stir until tender. Stir in remaining ingredients except chives.
Cover and simmer over low heat until heated through, 3 to 5 minutes.
Garnish with reserved bacon and chives, if desired. Serves 4 to 6.

Parsleyed Green Beans

Kim Warren
Hodgenville, KY

*I wanted a different way to serve garden-fresh green beans,
and found and adapted this recipe. It's always a hit because
the flavors really complement the beans.*

1-1/2 lbs. green beans, trimmed
3 T. oil
1/2 c. onion or green onion,
    diced
2 T. lemon juice

2 t. fresh thyme, chopped
1/2 t. Italian seasoning
1/2 c. fresh flat-leaf parsley,
    chopped
salt and pepper to taste

Steam or microwave beans until crisp-tender; drain. Set aside and keep
warm. Heat oil in a skillet and sauté onion until tender. Stir in lemon
juice and seasonings. Add beans to skillet and toss to coat; add salt
and pepper to taste. Serves 6.

Pork Chops Dijon

Abigail Smith
Gooseberry Patch

Super-easy and so flavorful.

3 T. Dijon mustard
2 T. Italian salad dressing
1/4 t. pepper

1 T. olive oil
4 pork loin chops
1 onion, thinly sliced

Combine mustard, salad dressing and pepper; set aside. Heat oil
in a skillet over medium-high heat. Brown pork chops on both sides;
remove from skillet. Add onion to skillet. Cook and stir over medium
heat for 3 minutes, until tender. Return pork chops to skillet; spread
with mustard mixture. Cover and cook over low heat for about
15 minutes. Serve pork chops topped with sauce from skillet.
Makes 4 servings.

German-Style Green Beans

Sharon Crider
Junction City, KS

This simple recipe turns canned beans into something special.

4 to 6 slices bacon, diced
1/3 c. onion, chopped
2 14-1/2 oz. cans green beans,
   drained

1/4 c. vinegar
2 T. sugar

In a skillet over medium heat, cook bacon until crisp. Drain bacon
and set aside; reserve 2 tablespoons drippings in skillet. Add onion
to drippings and sauté until tender. Stir in remaining ingredients;
cook until heated through. Stir in reserved bacon. Serves 8.

A quick side to serve with pork...sprinkle a teaspoon of
cinnamon into a can of apple pie filling. Cook over low heat
until warm and bubbly.

Sweet-and-Sour Pork Chops

Teri Lindquist
Gurnee, IL

We just love caramelized onions, so I decided to combine them with pork chops one day and it was a big hit! The sweet, tangy onions are enriched by the flavor of the pork. I've been making this for 10 years and it's still one of our favorite pork chop meals.

3 to 4 T. olive oil
4 sweet onions, thickly sliced
1/2 t. pepper

4 to 6 pork chops
1/4 c. brown sugar, packed
1/4 c. cider vinegar

Heat oil in a large skillet over medium heat. Add onion slices and sprinkle with pepper. Cook onions, stirring frequently, until golden and caramelized, about 15 to 20 minutes. Push onions to one side; add pork chops to skillet. Brown pork chops for one minute on each side. Spoon onions over pork chops. Mix together brown sugar and vinegar; drizzle over top. Simmer, stirring frequently, until sugar is dissolved, onions are well coated with sauce and pork chops are cooked through. Makes 4 to 6 servings.

Turn leftover mashed potatoes into crispy potato pancakes...
a delicious addition to any meal. Stir an egg yolk and some
minced onion into 2 cups potatoes. Form into patties and fry
in a little butter until golden...yum!

193

Mom's Chicken Riggies

Justine Hutchings
New York Mills, NY

I am from central New York and "Riggies" are a very popular dish here. My mother taught me how to make this quick & easy recipe...it is always a hit at any family gathering or party!

16-oz. pkg. rigatoni pasta, uncooked
2 to 3 T. oil
2 T. garlic, minced
2 boneless, skinless chicken breasts, cubed

8-oz. pkg. sliced mushrooms
1 green pepper, diced
26-oz. jar spaghetti sauce
Optional: 1/2 to 1 c. white wine
1 pt. whipping cream, divided

Cook pasta according to package directions; drain. While pasta is cooking, add oil to a skillet; sauté garlic over medium heat until golden. Add chicken; sauté until lightly golden. Add mushrooms and pepper; sauté until tender and soft. Stir to mix well; reduce heat to low. Pour sauce into a separate saucepan. Add wine, if using, and heat through. Stir in cream in small amounts until sauce becomes orange in color. Add to chicken mixture in skillet; stir to mix. Place cooked pasta in a large serving bowl. Top with sauce mixture and toss to mix all together. Serves 10 to 12.

Feel free to mix & match plates and glasses...create a casual look that's more fun than carefully matched tableware.

Chicken & Broccoli Alfredo

Patricia Ogilsbie
Canastota, NY

I like to cook boneless chicken breasts and cut them up to freeze in bags of 2-cup quantities, which makes meals like this one a snap to fix. Dinner is ready in about 30 minutes!

12-oz. pkg. penne pasta,
  uncooked and divided
2 c. broccoli flowerets, chopped
2 c. cooked chicken, cubed
2 T. olive oil

1-1/4 c. chicken broth, divided
4-oz. can sliced mushrooms,
  drained
1/4 t. pepper
16-oz. jar Alfredo sauce

Cook half of pasta according to package directions, reserving the remainder for another recipe. Set aside. In a deep frying pan, sauté broccoli and chicken in oil. Add one cup broth, mushrooms and pepper. Cover and cook for 5 to 7 minutes, until broccoli is tender. Add sauce to skillet. Pour remaining broth into empty sauce jar, shake and add to skillet. Simmer for 5 to 10 minutes. Stir in cooked pasta; return to a boil before serving. Serves 6.

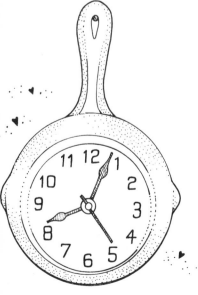

Make a whimsical wall clock from a vintage skillet in just minutes. Craft stores have clock kits with all the parts you need. Drill the center hole, insert the clock movement and hands, then press on self-adhesive numbers. Time for dinner!

Farmers' Market Stir-Fry

Jenny Nangoy
Austin, TX

This Asian-style recipe takes as little as 30 minutes to prepare. I adapted it to use ingredients that are easy to find here in the US. Use as many kinds of veggies as you like!

3 T. oil
3 to 4 cloves garlic, minced
1/2 lb. medium shrimp, cleaned
1/2 lb. boneless chicken, cut into 1-inch pieces
1/2 lb. boneless pork, cut into 1-inch pieces
2 carrots, peeled, quartered and cut into 1-inch pieces
3/4 c. green beans, cut into 1-inch pieces
3/4 c. peas
1-1/4 c. broccoli flowerets
1-1/4 c. cauliflower flowerets

3/4 c. onion, chopped
3/4 c. red, yellow or green peppers, cut into wedges
15 mushrooms, halved
8-oz. can sliced bamboo shoots, drained
6 green cabbage leaves, chopped
12 Chinese cabbage leaves, chopped
soy sauce to taste
salt and white pepper to taste
1 T. cornstarch
1 c. cold water
steamed rice

In a large wok or skillet, heat oil over medium-high heat. Add garlic; cook and stir for 30 seconds, until golden. Add shrimp, chicken and pork; cook and stir over high heat for 2 to 3 minutes, until well done. Add carrots; stir until partially cooked. Add remaining vegetables, soy sauce, salt and pepper. Cook, stirring constantly, until heated through. Dissolve cornstarch in water; add to skillet. Continue to cook and stir until thickened and all ingredients are tender. Serve over steamed rice. Makes 4 to 5 servings.

The secret to tasty stir-fries... slice everything into equal-size pieces before you start cooking! They'll all be cooked to perfection at the same time.

Tropical Chicken Stir-Fry
Vickie

This dish is so yummy and cooks up in a jiffy...it's a little taste of the islands! I like to serve scoops of orange sherbet and coconut ice cream for a sweet end to dinner.

1/4 c. soy sauce
2 T. sugar
1 T. cider vinegar
1 T. catsup
1 T. garlic, minced
1 t. cornstarch
1/2 t. ground ginger
8-oz. can pineapple chunks, drained and 1/4 c. juice reserved

2 T. oil
1 lb. boneless, skinless chicken breasts, sliced into strips
16-oz. pkg. frozen stir-fry vegetables, thawed
cooked rice
Optional: sliced almonds

In a bowl, mix first 7 ingredients and reserved pineapple juice; set aside. Heat oil in a skillet over medium-high heat. Add chicken; cook and stir for 5 minutes, until nearly done. Add vegetables; cook and stir for 4 minutes. Stir in pineapple and soy sauce mixture; heat through. Serve over cooked rice; sprinkle with almonds if desired. Serves 6.

Make a crystal flower vase sparkle! Fill it half full of hot water, then add a cup of uncooked rice, two tablespoons of white vinegar and a few drops of liquid dishwashing soap. Swirl the water around for a minute or two, rinse well and let dry.

Chicken-Mushroom Hash

Amy Butcher
Columbus, GA

If you like mushrooms, you'll love this made-from-scratch hash.

4 T. oil, divided
1 onion, chopped
2 cloves garlic, chopped
1/2 lb. mushrooms, chopped
1-1/4 lbs. boneless, skinless
   chicken breasts, cubed
1/2 t. dried thyme

1 t. salt, divided
1/4 t. pepper
2 lbs. potatoes, peeled, cubed
   and cooked
1/4 c. whipping cream
2 T. fresh parsley, chopped

In a large skillet over medium heat, heat one tablespoon oil. Add onion, garlic and mushrooms. Cook, stirring occasionally, until mushrooms are golden, 5 to 7 minutes. Add chicken, thyme, 1/2 teaspoon salt and pepper to skillet. Cook, stirring frequently, until chicken is almost done, 3 to 4 minutes. Drain; transfer mixture to a bowl. Add remaining oil to skillet over medium-high heat. Add potatoes; cook without stirring for about 6 minutes. Sprinkle with remaining salt; stir potatoes and cook until crisp and dark golden, about 4 minutes. Stir in chicken mixture, cream and parsley; heat through. Serves 4 to 6.

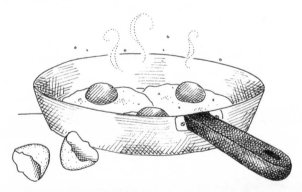

Top portions of hash with a poached egg...tasty for dinner or brunch. Fill a skillet with water and bring to a simmer. Swirl the water with a spoon and gently slide in an egg from a saucer. Let cook until set, about 2 minutes, and remove with a slotted spoon.

Chicken-Sausage Skilletini

Elizabeth Cisneros
Chino Hills, CA

Serve with French bread and olive oil for dipping.

1/4 c. olive oil
2 boneless, skinless chicken
   breasts, cubed
1/2 lb. spicy ground pork
   sausage
1 red onion, thinly sliced
2 cloves garlic, minced
14-1/2 oz. can diced tomatoes

1 red pepper, sliced
3 T. brown sugar, packed
1 t. dried basil
1/2 t. dried oregano
1/8 t. salt
1/8 t. pepper
16-oz. pkg. linguine pasta,
   cooked

Heat oil in a large skillet over medium heat. Add chicken, sausage,
onion and garlic; cook until meats are browned. Drain; add remaining
ingredients except pasta and simmer for 5 minutes. Add cooked pasta
to skillet and mix all ingredients together. Simmer another 5 minutes,
until pasta is heated through. Serves 4.

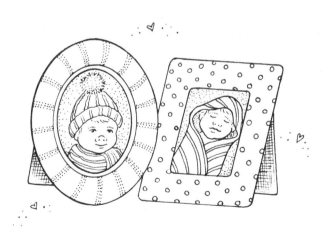

Mark each family member's place at dinner with a baby picture
placed in a mini picture frame...so sweet!

Taco Skillet Supper

Linda Nielsen
British Columbia, Canada

A nice twist on tacos served in a shell! Adjust the seasonings to your own family's preference.

1 lb. lean ground beef
1 onion, chopped
16-oz. can refried beans
4-oz. can chopped green chiles
1/4 to 1/2 t. garlic powder
1/2 to 1 t. chili powder
1/2 to 1 t. ground cumin
3/4 c. sour cream

8-oz. pkg. tortilla chips
1 tomato, chopped
1 green pepper, chopped
2-1/4 oz. can sliced black olives, drained
8-oz. pkg. shredded Mexican-blend cheese
Garnish: shredded lettuce, salsa

Brown beef and onion in a skillet over medium heat; drain. Stir in beans, chiles and garlic powder; heat through. Combine chili powder and cumin; sprinkle over beef mixture. Sour cream may be stirred in at this point, or may be served separately as a topping. To serve, spoon mixture over tortilla chips. Top with remaining ingredients. Serves 4 to 6.

White paper coffee filters are great for serving up tacos, wraps and burgers...no spills, no mess and easy for little hands to hold! Afterwards, just toss them away.

Chili Mac Skillet

Cherie White
Oklahoma City, OK

This cheesy dinner is so quick & easy, you don't even have to cook the macaroni separately!

1 onion, chopped
1 to 2 t. oil
1 lb. ground beef
seasoning salt to taste
8-oz. pkg. elbow macaroni,
    uncooked and divided
15-oz. can kidney beans,
    drained and rinsed

8-oz. can tomato sauce
4-oz. can diced green chiles
1/4 c. water
1 T. chili powder
1/2 t. garlic powder
1 c. shredded Cheddar cheese

In a skillet over medium heat, sauté onion in oil. Add beef and seasoning salt. Cook until beef is browned; drain. Measure out 1/2 cup macaroni and add to skillet; set aside remaining macaroni for another use. Stir in remaining ingredients except cheese. Bring to a boil; reduce heat. Cover and simmer for 20 minutes, stirring often, until macaroni is tender. Remove from heat; sprinkle with cheese, cover and let stand until cheese is melted, about 2 minutes. Makes 4 to 6 servings.

Mmm...fresh air always makes us hungry! One-dish skillet suppers are perfect for a campfire cookout. Save time by chopping the veggies at home and placing them in small bags for the cooler. Or choose a recipe with mostly canned ingredients...don't forget the can-opener!

One-Pot Pork Chop Supper

Julie Ball
Portland, MI

This simple recipe holds such great memories for me. I have my mother's recipe card, typed by her on an old-fashioned ribbon typewriter, and the card is now yellowed from so much use. Be sure to serve with some bread to soak up the wonderful gravy...yummy!

1 onion, sliced
8 pork chops
2 to 3 T. oil
8 potatoes, peeled and quartered
8 carrots, peeled, halved
   lengthwise and cut into
   2-inch pieces

2 10-3/4 oz. cans tomato soup
1 c. water
2 T. Worcestershire sauce
2 t. dried oregano
1 t. salt
1/2 t. pepper

In a very large skillet over medium heat, cook onion and pork chops in oil until browned. Drain; add potatoes and carrots to skillet. Mix remaining ingredients and pour into skillet. Cover; reduce heat and simmer for one hour, until pork chops are tender. Makes 8 servings.

Honey butter is scrumptious on fresh-baked biscuits and bread.
Simply blend 1/2 cup each of honey and softened butter
and spoon into a small crock.

Honey Chicken & Carrots

Coleen Lambert
Luxemburg, WI

This takes about 15 minutes to make and is so good. I cook a couple of boil-in-bags of rice alongside...dinner is ready in a jiffy!

1 T. oil	2 T. honey
4 boneless, skinless chicken breasts	1 T. lemon juice
	1/4 t. garlic salt
1-1/2 c. carrots, peeled and sliced	salt and pepper to taste
	cooked rice

Heat oil in a skillet over medium heat. Add chicken; cook until golden and juices run clear. Remove chicken from skillet; keep warm. Add carrots to skillet; cook for 3 to 5 minutes, or until tender. Stir in honey, lemon juice and garlic salt. Return chicken to skillet. Add salt and pepper to taste; heat to a boil. To serve, spoon over cooked rice. Serves 4.

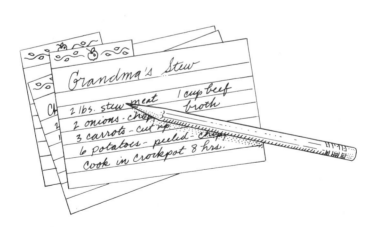

A thoughtful gift for a new bride who's just learning to cook. Jot down several favorite, tried & true recipes on individual cards... tuck them into a shiny new skillet along with a spatula and a wire whisk. Wrap it all up in a pretty tea towel...she'll love it!

Aunt Mary's Skillet Chicken

Terri Witkowski
Reading, PA

This recipe is from my Great-Aunt Mary and is a simple dish with a wonderful flavor. It's the best thing my mother has ever made...so needless to say, it is now in my own recipe box too!

4 boneless, skinless chicken
   breasts
3 T. grated Parmesan cheese
1/3 c. all-purpose flour
salt and pepper to taste
2 T. olive oil
1 c. sliced mushrooms

1 onion, finely chopped
1 clove garlic, minced
2 14-1/2 oz. cans Italian-
   seasoned diced tomatoes
1 t. Italian seasoning
1 t. dried parsley
7-oz. pkg. spaghetti, cooked

Place chicken breasts between 2 pieces of wax paper; pound to flatten slightly. Mix cheese, flour, salt and pepper; coat chicken in mixture. Heat oil in a skillet over medium heat. Cook chicken until tender and juices run clear, about 10 minutes on each side. Remove chicken to a serving dish; keep warm. In same skillet, cook mushrooms, onion and garlic until tender, about 5 minutes. Stir in tomatoes, seasoning and parsley. Simmer, uncovered, over medium heat until thickened and flavors blend. Serve chicken on spaghetti, topped with sauce. Serves 4.

Looking to reduce fat and calories? In skillet recipes that start with browning the meat, oil can usually be replaced with a few sprays of non-stick vegetable spray.

Linguine & Vegetables

Elaine Nichols
Mesa, AZ

This super-quick dish is a great alternative to the usual pasta & tomato sauce...give it a try and I think you'll agree!

1 T. olive oil
16-oz. pkg. linguine pasta, uncooked and broken up
1/2 c. onion, finely chopped
2 cloves garlic, minced
1 T. Italian seasoning
salt and pepper to taste
2 14-oz. cans vegetable broth, divided

14-1/2 oz. can Italian-seasoned diced tomatoes, drained
16-oz. pkg. frozen Italian-blend vegetables
4-oz. can button mushrooms, drained
Garnish: grated Parmesan cheese

Heat oil in a large skillet over medium heat. Add uncooked linguine; cook and stir until golden. Add onion, garlic and seasonings; simmer for about 5 minutes. Stir in one can broth and simmer until linguine is tender, adding the other can as needed. Add all vegetables; simmer until vegetables are tender. Drain; sprinkle with cheese before serving. Serves 6.

Give whole-wheat pasta a try in your favorite pasta recipe... it contains more fiber than regular pasta and tastes great too.

Spanish Paella

Rhonda Reeder
Ellicott City, MD

Make it extra special...add 1/2 pound frozen shrimp along with the chicken and cook until it turns pink.

3-1/2 oz. pkg. sliced pepperoni
1 T. oil
1 lb. boneless, skinless chicken
   breasts, cubed
1 red pepper, diced
1 clove garlic, pressed

1-1/2 t. dried thyme
8-oz. pkg. Spanish-style yellow
   rice mix, uncooked
2 c. water
10-oz. pkg. frozen peas

In a skillet or wok over medium-high heat, cook pepperoni for 2 to 3 minutes, stirring occasionally. Remove pepperoni to a plate; set aside. Add oil and chicken to skillet. Cook 3 to 4 minutes, until juices run clear. Drain; remove chicken to a plate. Add red pepper, garlic and thyme to skillet; cook and stir for one minute. Stir in rice mix, water and pepperoni; heat mixture to boiling. Reduce heat to medium-low; cover and simmer for 10 minutes, until rice is nearly tender. Stir in frozen peas; cover again and cook for 5 minutes, covered. Return chicken to skillet; heat through. Serves 4.

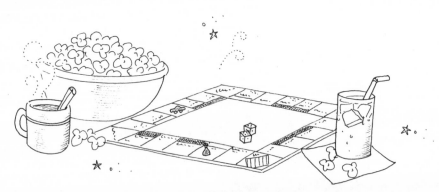

Invite family & friends over for a Game Night. After enjoying a casual supper together, bring out all the old favorite board games. Don't forget to supply silly prizes and big bowls of buttered popcorn as the evening goes on!

Amanda's Chicken & Orzo

Cathy Gearheart
Narrows, VA

A great quick meal in about 20 minutes. This was a staple when my daughter was involved in sports and needed a light, quick, nutritious meal before a game.

4 T. olive oil, divided
4 boneless, skinless chicken
  breasts
1 t. dried basil
salt and pepper to taste
2 zucchini, sliced

8-oz. pkg. orzo pasta, uncooked
1 T. butter, softened
2 T. red wine vinegar
Optional: 1 t. fresh dill, snipped
Garnish: lemon wedges

Heat 2 tablespoons oil in a skillet. Sprinkle chicken with basil, salt and pepper. Add to skillet and cook for 12 minutes, or until juices run clear, turning once. Remove chicken to a plate; keep warm. Add zucchini to skillet and cook for 3 minutes, or until crisp-tender. Meanwhile, cook orzo according to package directions; drain and stir in butter. Whisk together remaining oil, vinegar and dill, if using; drizzle over orzo and toss to mix. Season with additional salt and pepper, as desired. Serve chicken and zucchini with orzo, garnished with lemon wedges. Serves 4.

Share the garden bounty! A market basket of seasonal veggies makes a terrific gift for a friend or neighbor.

Gingered Broccoli Beef

Regina Wickline
Pebble Beach, CA

The list of ingredients may look long, but this one-dish meal goes together very quickly. Try it with boneless chicken or pork too.

1 bunch broccoli, cut into
   flowerets
1 lb. beef tenderloin, sliced into
   thin strips
1 T. fresh ginger, peeled and
   grated
3 cloves garlic, pressed

1/4 t. red pepper flakes
1 to 2 t. olive oil
3/4 c. chicken broth
3 T. soy sauce
1 T. cornstarch
1/2 t. sesame oil

Cover broccoli with water in a saucepan. Bring to a boil and cook until crisp-tender, about 3 to 5 minutes. Drain; set aside and cover to keep warm. Toss beef with ginger, garlic and red pepper flakes. Add oil to a skillet over medium-high heat. Add beef mixture and cook for 2 to 3 minutes, stirring constantly, until beef is lightly browned. Whisk together remaining ingredients and add to skillet; heat to boiling. Cook and stir for one minute, or until sauce thickens slightly. Add broccoli and toss to coat. Makes 4 servings.

Speedy supper! In the morning, combine uncooked pork chops, beef strips or chicken cutlets with marinade in plastic zipping bags and refrigerate. At dinnertime, the pre-seasoned meat can pop right into the skillet for a scrumptious meal in a jiffy.

"Leftover" Fried Rice

Kim Ah Mu
Independence, MO

This is a great way to make a yummy meal with all those little bits of leftovers in the fridge. Some like just a little soy sauce, but we like the rice to be all brown in color.

2 to 3 t. oil
4 eggs, beaten
1 to 2 c. leftover cooked chicken
  or pork, diced
3 to 4 c. cooked rice
soy sauce or teriyaki sauce
  to taste

1 to 2 c. leftover cooked
  vegetables like broccoli,
  carrots and peas
Optional: garlic powder, salt
  and pepper to taste

Heat oil in a skillet over medium-low heat. Add eggs; scramble lightly. Add meat and heat through, stirring frequently. Add rice and sauce; continue cooking and stirring. Add vegetables; stir to mix well and heat through. Season to taste with garlic powder, salt and pepper, if desired. Serve immediately. Serves 4 to 6.

A super-simple, whimsical dessert to serve after an Asian meal!
Scoop rainbow sherbet into stemmed glasses, then slip
a fortune cookie over the edge of each glass.

Slam-Together Goulash

Jeannie Phillips
Troy, MI

My mom, Ginny, a true Southern cook, had a way of making everything taste delicious. She always just called this dish "Slam-Together," since she took kitchen staples and put them together quickly to make a great meal. You'll have people asking for seconds!

2 T. olive oil	3 cloves garlic, minced
2 onions, diced	1 t. Italian seasoning
2 c. celery, diced	1 t. salt
2 carrots, diced	16-oz. pkg. elbow macaroni,
1 lb. lean ground beef	uncooked
46-oz. can cocktail vegetable	1 c. shredded 3-cheese blend
juice	Optional: hot pepper sauce
14-1/2 oz. Italian-seasoned	
stewed tomatoes	

Heat oil in a large deep skillet over medium heat. Add onions, celery and carrots; sauté until onions are translucent. Add beef and cook until browned; drain. Stir in vegetable juice, tomatoes with juice, garlic and seasonings. Bring to a boil. Add uncooked macaroni; return to a boil. Cover and cook until macaroni is tender, about 10 minutes. Remove from heat; stir in cheese and hot sauce, if desired. Serves 8.

Show off the bright colors of a fruit salad by serving it in old-fashioned glass compotes.

Alysha's Veggie Rice

Jean DePerna
Fairport, NY

*I started making this dish when my daughter was younger,
as a tasty way to get her to eat veggies. We still enjoy it
often as a quick & easy meal.*

1 lb. ground beef or ground
   turkey
2 c. water
1 cube beef or chicken bouillon
1-1/2 c. favorite vegetables,
   chopped

1 c. instant brown rice,
   uncooked
salt and pepper to taste

In a skillet over medium heat, brown beef or turkey; drain. Add water
and bouillon to skillet; stir until bouillon is dissolved. Add remaining
ingredients. Bring to a boil; reduce heat to low. Cover and simmer
until liquid is absorbed and rice is fluffy and tender, about 15 to
20 minutes. Serves 4.

Why not "adopt" an older neighbor or friend as a grandparent?
Include him or her in the children's ball games and family
outings...bake cookies together and share stories over dinner. Your
family can help out by weeding flower beds, raking leaves and
running errands for them...it's sure to be rewarding for everybody!

Hamburger Gravy

Jasmine Burgess
East Lansing, MI

My mom was a busy working mother who held down two jobs while raising four kids, so we all learned to cook early! This yummy recipe was a weekly favorite...it's easy to change by serving it over pasta, rice, potatoes or even pierogies.

1 lb. lean ground beef
1/2 c. onion, diced
1 t. garlic, pressed
1 t. salt
10-3/4 oz. can cream of
   mushroom soup
10-3/4 oz. can cream of
   chicken soup

1 c. milk
1 c. light sour cream
1 t. paprika
1 t. dried thyme or herbes
   de Provence
cooked egg noodles

Brown beef with onion, garlic and salt in a skillet over medium heat. Drain; add soups, milk, sour cream and seasonings. Stir to combine. Heat until bubbly and as thick as desired. Serve over cooked noodles. Makes 4 to 6 servings.

Need a quick side dish in a hurry? Dress up a package of refrigerated mashed potatoes. Heat as directed, then stir in a dollop of chive-flavored cream cheese and top with bacon bits.

E-Z California Stroganoff

Cynthia Dodge
Layton, UT

This recipe came from sheer necessity one day...money was in short supply and the kids were hungry! So I stirred this up using what was on hand in the fridge and pantry. Everyone loved it!

1/2 to 3/4 lb. lean ground beef	2 c. milk
1/2 t. seasoned salt with onion & garlic	2 3-oz. pkgs. beef or mushroom-flavored ramen noodles, divided
1/2 t. salt-free herb seasoning	
1/2 t. garlic powder	2 c. frozen California-blend vegetables
1/2 t. onion powder	
3/4 c. hot water	1/2 c. frozen corn

In a skillet or wok over medium heat, brown beef with seasonings; drain. Add hot water, milk and seasoning packets from noodles. Stir to mix well. Add vegetables. Continue cooking over medium heat, stirring frequently, for about 5 minutes. Crush noodles and add to beef mixture; stir to blend thoroughly. Reduce heat to low. Simmer until noodles are tender and vegetables are heated through. Serves 6.

Decorate a reusable shopping bag for toting home groceries... it's so easy, you'll want to make several. Pick up a plain canvas tote bag from a craft store and and attach a big square of pretty fabric to each side with simple stitching or fabric glue.

Tuscan Rosemary Chicken

Cherylann Smith
Efland, NC

*This one-dish dinner is so flavorful, no one will guess
how easy it is to fix!*

1/3 c. balsamic vinaigrette
  salad dressing
4 boneless, skinless chicken
  breasts
1/4 c. water
1 c. baby carrots, sliced
2 stalks celery, sliced

1/4 c. sun-dried tomato pesto
1 T. Italian seasoning
1 to 2 T. fresh rosemary,
  chopped
2 15-oz. cans navy beans,
  drained and rinsed

In a skillet, heat salad dressing over medium-high heat. Add chicken
to skillet. Cook for 2 to 3 minutes on each side, until lightly golden.
Reduce heat to medium-low. Add remaining ingredients except beans.
Cover; simmer for about 10 minutes, or until carrots are crisp-tender
and chicken juices run clear. Stir in beans. Simmer over low heat for
30 minutes, stirring occasionally. Serves 6.

Give tossed salads extra flavor and crunch with a sprinkle of
toasted nuts...it's easy. Place chopped walnuts or pecans in a small
dry skillet. Cook and stir over low heat for a few minutes until
toasty and golden. Let cool before adding to salads.

Hannah's Lemon Chicken & Bows

Linda Roth
Windsor Heights, IA

My daughter loves lemons and we eat lots of chicken, so I created this recipe especially for her. We like this dish with cooked peas or broccoli mixed in as well.

1 onion, finely chopped
4 cloves garlic, minced
2 T. olive oil
4 to 5 boneless, skinless
   chicken breasts, cubed
salt and pepper to taste
2 T. lemon zest, divided
2 t. dried basil

1/2 c. butter
1/2 c. all-purpose flour
6 T. lemon juice
4 c. chicken broth
16-oz. pkg. bowtie pasta,
   cooked
Garnish: shredded Parmesan
   cheese

In a skillet over medium heat, sauté onion and garlic in oil for about 5 minutes. Add chicken, salt and pepper. When chicken is partially done, stir in one tablespoon lemon zest and basil. Continue to sauté until thoroughly cooked. Meanwhile, in a saucepan over medium heat, melt butter. Stir in flour and cook until bubbly. Add lemon juice, broth and remaining zest to saucepan. Cook until sauce begins to bubble and thicken. To serve, pour sauce over cooked pasta. Add chicken and mix to coat evenly. Garnish with cheese. Serves 6.

For the freshest flavor, olive oil should be stored in the fridge...just pour a little into a small cruet for everyday use. Olive oil thickens when chilled, but will thin quickly at room temperature.

Burger Skillet Casserole

Andrea Nesselhauf
Erie, PA

I learned to make this in high school when electric skillets were all the rage. It's a great weeknight meal with fresh-baked bread and some zesty bread & butter pickles.

1 lb. ground beef, turkey or
  chicken
1 onion, diced
chili powder, salt and pepper
  to taste

28-oz. can diced tomatoes
12-oz. pkg. wide egg noodles,
  uncooked and divided
11-oz. can corn, drained
6 slices American cheese

In a skillet over medium heat, brown meat with onion and seasonings. Drain; stir in tomatoes with juice. Add half the package of egg noodles; reserve remaining noodles for another recipe. Cover skillet and cook until noodles are tender, about 7 to 10 minutes. Stir in corn and heat through. Arrange cheese slices on top. Cover again for a few minutes, until cheese is melted. Makes 4 servings.

When tacos, hamburgers, hot dogs or baked potatoes are on the menu, set up a topping bar with bowls of shredded cheese, salsa, guacamole, crispy bacon and other yummy garnishes. Everyone can just help themselves by adding their favorite toppings to individual servings.

One-Pot Sausage Dinner

Crystal Hamlett
Amory, MS

This is one of my go-to recipes when time is short on a busy day.
The sausage flavor cooks into the other ingredients...yum!

1 lb. smoked pork sausage,
  sliced
1 head cabbage, coarsely
  chopped
14-1/2 oz. Italian green beans,
  drained

2 15-oz. cans sliced new
  potatoes, drained
1 onion, sliced
1/2 to 1 c. water
salt and pepper to taste
1/2 c. butter, sliced

Brown sausage lightly in a large deep skillet or saucepan; drain. Layer
with cabbage, beans, potatoes and onion. Sprinkle with water, salt
and pepper; dot with butter. Cover and cook over medium-high heat
until cabbage starts to wilt, about 5 minutes. Reduce heat and cook
until tender, about 5 to 10 additional minutes. Makes 4 servings.

Just for fun, serve up beverages
at dinner in vintage half-pint
milk bottles. Don't forget the
bendy straws!

Spicy Shrimp Noodle Bowl

Laura Witham
Anchorage, AK

Whenever my husband and I go out for Asian food, my favorite dishes are the noodle bowls. Here is my own version of a satisfying, spicy shrimp noodle bowl that you can make at home.

3 T. olive oil
1 leek, chopped
4 cloves garlic, minced
2 t. red pepper flakes
salt and pepper to taste
4 c. chicken broth

2 8-oz. bottles clam juice
8-oz. pkg. angel hair pasta, uncooked
1 lb. uncooked medium shrimp, peeled and cleaned

Heat a large deep skillet over medium heat; add oil. Add leek and seasonings; sauté for 3 minutes. Pour in broth and juice; bring to a boil. Turn down to a simmer. Add pasta to skillet and cook for 3 to 5 minutes, until tender. Add shrimp and cook 5 minutes more. Serve immediately. Serves 4 to 6.

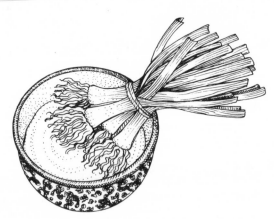

Leeks are delicious in recipes but are frequently sandy when purchased. To quickly clean leeks, slice them into 2-inch lengths and soak in a bowl of cold water. Swish them in the water and drain. Refill the bowl and swish again until the water is clear. Drain and pat dry...they're recipe-ready!

Green Pepper Vermicelli

Isolda Crockett
Mossville, IL

We have five active children. It is so wonderful to take time each night,
sit around the table together with all the noise and laughter
and share dinner together...what a blessing!

1 onion, minced
1 clove garlic, minced
2 T. olive oil
3 T. butter
4 green peppers, diced
1 c. chicken broth

1 t. salt
pepper to taste
16-oz. pkg. vermicelli pasta,
   cooked
Garnish: 1/4 c. shredded Asiago
   cheese

In a skillet over medium heat, sauté onion and garlic in oil and
butter until onion is softened. Add green peppers and simmer for
10 minutes. Stir in broth, salt and pepper; mix well and simmer for
15 minutes. To serve, add sauce to cooked pasta and toss well.
Sprinkle with cheese. Serves 6.

Pick up some paper plates, cups and napkins in seasonal
designs...they'll make dinner fun when time is short
and clean-up will be a breeze.

Slow Cookers

Casseroles

Skillets

Send us your favorite recipe!

and the memory that makes it special for you!* If we select your recipe for a brand-new **Gooseberry Patch** cookbook, your name will appear right along with it...and you'll receive a FREE copy of the book.

Share your recipe on our website at
www.gooseberrypatch.com

Or mail to:

Gooseberry Patch • Attn: Cookbook Dept.
P.O. Box 190 • Delaware, OH 43015

*Don't forget to include your name, address, phone number and email address so we'll know how to reach you for your FREE book!

Since 1992, we've been publishing country cookbooks for every kitchen and for every meal of the day! Each has hundreds of budget-friendly recipes, using ingredients you already have on hand. Their lay-flat binding makes them easy to use and each is filled with hand-drawn artwork and plenty of personality.

Have a taste for more?

Call us toll-free at

1•800•854•6673

Find us here too!

Join our **Circle of Friends** and discover free recipes & crafts, plus giveaways & more! Visit our website or blog to join and be sure to follow us on Facebook & Twitter!

www.gooseberrypatch.com

Join Our Circle of Friends

VIDEOS

Read Our **Blog**

Find us on Facebook

Follow us on **twitter**

U.S. to Canadian recipe equivalents

Volume Measurements

1/4 teaspoon	1 mL
1/2 teaspoon	2 mL
1 teaspoon	5 mL
1 tablespoon = 3 teaspoons	15 mL
2 tablespoons = 1 fluid ounce	30 mL
1/4 cup	60 mL
1/3 cup	75 mL
1/2 cup = 4 fluid ounces	125 mL
1 cup = 8 fluid ounces	250 mL
2 cups = 1 pint =16 fluid ounces	500 mL
4 cups = 1 quart	1 L

Weights

1 ounce	30 g
4 ounces	120 g
8 ounces	225 g
16 ounces = 1 pound	450 g

Oven Temperatures

300° F	150° C
325° F	160° C
350° F	180° C
375° F	190° C
400° F	200° C
450° F	230° C

Baking Pan Sizes

Square
8x8x2 inches	2 L = 20x20x5 cm
9x9x2 inches	2.5 L = 23x23x5 cm

Rectangular
13x9x2 inches	3.5 L = 33x23x5 cm

Loaf
9x5x3 inches	2 L = 23x13x7 cm

Round
8x1-1/2 inches	1.2 L = 20x4 cm
9x1-1/2 inches	1.5 L = 23x4 cm